The Complete Cotswolds

A COMPREHENSIVE GUIDE WITH 26 SPECIALLY PREPARED MAPS AND OVER 350 ILLUSTRATIONS

By PETER, HELEN
and DAVID
TITCHMARSH

Photography by
Alan and Peter
Titchmarsh

MARKET HALL, CHIPPING CAMPDEN

Published by: Jarrolds Colour Publications, Barrack Street, Norwich
© P. A. Titchmarsh

1 Western Edge Country 6– 9
2 The Far South West 10–13
3 Cloth Valleys and Western
   Beacons 14–17
4 Deep Valleys and Broad
   Uplands 18–21
5 Western Slopes and a
   Southern River 22–27
6 Gentle Valleys, Great
   Woodlands and an Old Canal 28–31
7 A Roman Valley and
   Medieval Abbeys 32– 37
8 Secret Woodlands and a
   Roman Villa 38–41
9 Roman Roads and the
   Birthplace of the Thames 42–45
10 Some North Cotswold
   Classics 46–51
11 Quiet Woodlands and the
   Stripling Windrush 52–55
12 Fosse Country and the
   Middle Coln 56–59
13 Southwards to the Thames 60–63
14 Chipping Campden and the
   Far North 64–67
15 High Wolds and a Delectable
   Brewery 68–73
16 The Middle Windrush and a
   Cotswold Mecca 74–77
17 The Lower Leach and Coln
   Valleys 78–81
18 Four Shires Country 82–87
19 The Broad Evenlode Valley 88–91
20 Windrush Country and a
   Wildlife Park 92–97
21 Red Horse Country and the
   Northern Edge 98–101
22 Heythrop Country and the
   Nortons 102–105
23 Wychwood Country and the
   Lower Windrush 106–109
24 Ironstone Country of the
   Far North East 110–113
25 Tewland and the Glyme
   Valley 114–117
26 The Churchill Country 118–121

KEY MAP

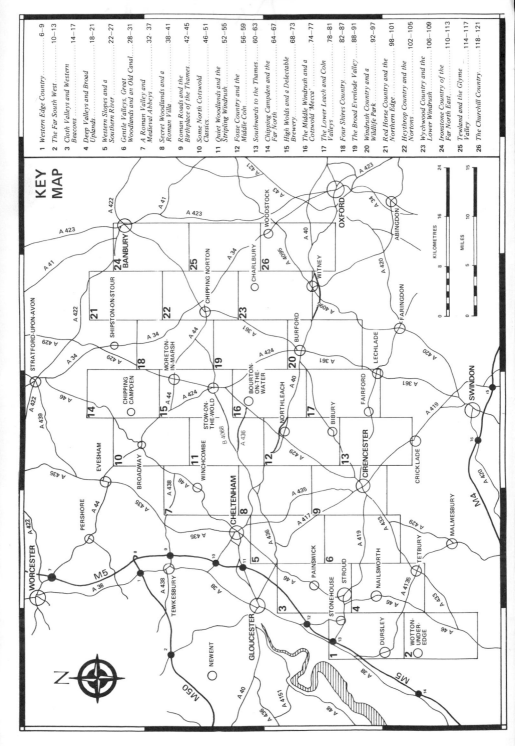

Introduction

This guide book is the result of several years' wandering in the Cotswolds, and will we hope, give some indication of the very wide variety of interest and beauty that this area contains. Some readers may feel that we have strayed too far, by including the country eastwards from Chipping Norton and southwards almost to the Thames. However when you have sampled these areas, we are sure you will agree with us that they are essentially Cotswold in feeling, and that they certainly deserve to be included. In our further defence we would refer you to H. J. Massingham's classic *Cotswold Country*, which includes all the wold country between Lincolnshire and Dorset within its covers.

We have tried to produce a simple guide book to the whole Cotswold area, in which it will be easy to track down any town, village or place of interest that you may wish to visit. At the same time we recognize that many people may wish to explore a particular area by car, bicycle or on foot, and we have therefore divided our guide into twenty-six self contained 'chapters', each with its own large scale map, depicting A, B and C roads, and some of the more interesting footpaths and bridle-ways.

To locate a particular town or village, first refer to the index at the rear of the guide. This will enable you to find the page on which the required entry will be found. This entry will be coded with the number of the map on which it appears, and with the particular quarter of the map in question (NW, NE, SW or SE). The map in question will be found at the beginning of the 'chapter' to which it refers, each 'chapter' being either four or six pages in length. The inevitable frustration of relating two or more maps to each other has been minimized by the inclusion of clear cross references on the map margins, and the provision of a simple outline Key Map.

We feel that our maps provide perfectly adequate guidance for motorists, but would advise those who wish to explore the Cotswolds on foot to make use of the Ordnance Survey's 1:50,000 Maps — Sheet Numbers 150, 151, 162, 163, 164, 172, or the O.S. Tourist Map of the Cotswolds at One Inch to the Mile, which covers most of the 'popular' area of the Cotswolds. If a particular area is to be explored in very great detail, the Ordnance Survey's 1:25,000 series (about 2½" to the mile) is to be recommended, but it would be expensive to purchase all the maps in this scale, to cover the whole Cotswold area. We are conscious of the fact that our own maps do not provide detailed guidance for the walker, but the selection of footpaths and bridle-ways which we have included will we hope, underline the immense opportunities offered to the walker in the Cotswolds. Reference to the Cotswold Way will be found on page 5.

Should you wish to follow a series of recommended routes, we would suggest that you make use of our companion guides, *Cotwolds by Car, Books 1, 2* and *3* (see inside front cover for details of the routes covered). However, with the help of the maps provided in this guide, you should have no difficulty in planning your own routes.

You will note that where ever possible, we have illustrated our descriptions with small black and white photographs, and in certain cases we have located these by a cross reference to the relevant map. We have also cross referenced certain items in the text with the relevant map, but for simplicity we have tried to keep both these references to a minimum.

We trust that we have not been guilty of any inaccuracies, but if any are discovered, we hope that you will not hesitate to draw our attention to them. We claim to have visited over ninety-five per cent of all places described, although in certain instances we have found churches locked, without any indication of the availability of the key. In view of vandalism and thievery we sympathise with those incumbents who feel it necessary to lock their churches, but would ask the minority amongst those who do so, to clearly indicate the address from which the key may be obtained.

The preparation of this guide has provided us with an excellent alibi for many hundreds of happy hours in Cotswold country, and we would like to express the wish that your own Cotswold wanderings will prove to be as enjoyable as our own. If you walk or cycle you require no further advice from us, but if you intend to travel by car, may we ask you to drive slowly and stop often...the Cotswolds are still wonderfully tranquil, and it is vital to us all, that they remain so.

PETER, HELEN and DAVID TITCHMARSH
Kineton, Warwick.

Springtime at Salperton — See Page 55.

The Cotswold Way

This is a ninety mile long route for walkers, along the Cotswold edge country between Chipping Campden and Bath. It was launched by Gloucestershire County Council in 1970, but has not yet achieved the status of a national 'long distance footpath'. It provides a fine walk taking between seven and nine days, although many people will wish to tackle portions of the route on separate days, especially if young families are involved. *A Guide to the Cotswold Way*, by Richard Searle (published by Constable) provides map coverage at 2½ inches to the mile, a series of excellent photographs and most informative text. You may however prefer to purchase the O.S. 1:50,000 maps, sheet numbers 150, 151, 162, 163 and 172, or for the Chipping Campden – Painswick section, the O.S. Tourist Map of the Cotswolds, at One Inch to the Mile.

Briefly, the route passes through the following places: CHIPPING CAMPDEN, BROADWAY, STANTON, STANWAY, HAILES ABBEY, WINCHCOMBE, BELAS KNAP, CLEEVE HILL, SEVEN SPRINGS, DEVIL'S CHIMNEY, CRICKLEY HILL, BARROW WAKE, BIRDLIP, WITCOMBE ROMAN VILLA, COOPER'S HILL, PAINSWICK BEACON, PAINSWICK, HARESFIELD BEACON, ROCESTER HILL, HETTY PEGLER'S TUMP, ULEYBURY, DURSLEY, STINCHCOMBE HILL, NORTH NIBLEY, TYNDALE MONUMENT, WOTTON-UNDER-EDGE, ALDERLEY, LOWER KILCOTT, SOMERSET MONUMENT, HAWKESBURY UPTON, HORTON COURT, LITTLE SODBURY, (now leaving the area covered by this guide) OLD SODBURY, TORMARTON, DODINGTON PARK, DYRHAM PARK, PENNSYLVANIA, COLD ASHTON, WESTON, BATH.

Apart from the route beyond Little Sodbury, all the places mentioned above are described in our guide, but we regret that we have not been able to describe the Cotswold Way in detail.

MAP SYMBOLS

Village with church .. .. **North Leigh ✚**	Hamlets	⋯⋯⋮
Town with church .. ..**WOODSTOCK ✚**	Water (lakes, reservoirs, etc.)	⬭
House or other features open to public .. ●	Motorways	▬▬▬
	A roads	▬▬▬
House or other features not open to public O	B roads	────
Antiquity .. .. .. *Long Barrow*	C roads	────
Earthworks .. .. ⊔⊔⊔⊔⊔	Footpaths and bridle-ways ..	─ ─ ─ ─

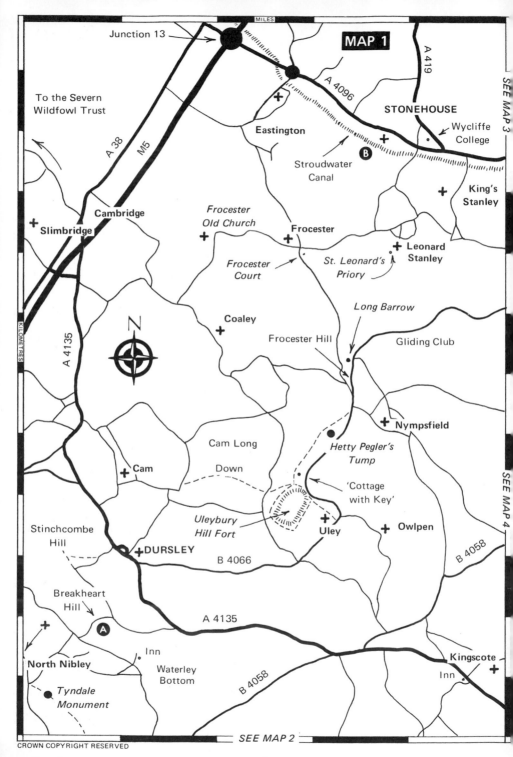

MILES

Junction 13

MAP 1

A 419

To the Severn
Wildfowl Trust

A 4096

STONEHOUSE

Wycliffe
College

Eastington

Stroudwater
Canal

B

A 38

M5

King's
Stanley

Cambridge

*Frocester
Old Church*

Frocester

+ Slimbridge

*Frocester
Court*

*St. Leonard's
Priory*

**+ Leonard
Stanley**

Long Barrow

Coaley

Frocester Hill

Gliding Club

N

A 4135

Nympsfield

KILOMETRES

Cam Long

*Hetty Pegler's
Tump*

+ Cam

Down

'Cottage
with Key'

*Uleybury
Hill Fort*

Uley

+ Owlpen

Stinchcombe
Hill

+ DURSLEY

B 4066

B 4058

Breakheart
Hill

A 4135

A

Inn

+ North Nibley

Waterley
Bottom

B 4058

Kingscote
+

Inn

*Tyndale
Monument*

SEE MAP 2

SEE MAP 3

SEE MAP 4

Map I

Western Edge Country

DURSLEY, OWLPEN, SLIMBRIDGE, STONEHOUSE, ULEY, etc....

CAM

(1–SW) (1 mile North of Dursley)
Large village in the industrialised valley of the Cam. One cloth mill remains, producing high quality 'West of England' cloth, used mainly for military uniforms and the cladding of billiard tables. Upper Cam church is a large building, believed to have been built by Lord Berkeley in the hope of saving his eternal soul, following the murder of Edward II. The interior was partially 'scraped' by the Victorians, but it contains a Jacobean pulpit on a slender base, a pleasant selection of 18th century wall monuments, and an unusual wall tablet to the Rev. W.C. Holder, with a model of his vicarage included.

In Cam Churchyard

COALEY

(1–NW) (2½ miles North East of Dursley)
Small village lying below the Cotswold edge. Flowering cherries line the churchyard path, which is overlooked by a finely pinnacled Perpendicular tower. The rest of the church was built in the 1850's and contains little of interest apart from an attractive 17th century brass depicting Daniel Stayno, complete with wife and children.

DURSLEY

(1–SW) (8 miles South West of Stroud)
Busy market town beneath the Cotswold edge, with extensive industry replacing the vanished cloth trade. It is centred upon a delightful 18th century Market House/Town Hall, complete with elegant statue of Queen Anne. The nearby church has a beautifully vaulted Perpendicular porch, but its interior has been disappointingly over-restored. The impressive tower was re-built in the Gothic style in 1709, and is only twenty years older than the Town Hall.

Town Hall, Dursley

EASTINGTON

(1 NW) (2 miles West of Stonehouse)
A rather scrappy village nearer the M 5 motorway than the Cotswold edge. However the church lies well away to the north east, in a large churchyard bordering on the River Frome, with flowering cherries on its banks. It has a 14th century tower, but is otherwise almost entirely Perpendicular, with handsome south aisle added by the Duke of Buckingham, shortly before his execution in 1521. This is a building full of interest, further enriched by the work of three of our favourite 20th century restorers: Sir Ninian Comper, S.E. Dykes-Bower and F.C. Eden.

Dursley Church

Blossom Time at Eastington

At Frocester Cross Roads

Frocester Hill

Breakheart Hill — Map Ref. **Ⓐ**

Romanesque Sculpture, Leonard Stanley

FROCESTER

(1—NE) (2 miles South West of Stonehouse)
Small village below the Cotswold edge, centred upon a
cross roads, which is overlooked by the Royal Gloucestershire Hussar, a pleasant, white painted inn. The
'new' church was largely re-built in the 19th century
and is not of great interest. The 'old' church is about a
mile to the west, and was finally demolished, in 1952
after a brief revival in the mid 19th century.....hence
the Victorian gothic tower and spire, which are now
all that survive. Medieval Frocester Court was owned
by the Abbey of Gloucester, and its tithe barn is one
of England's finest specimens, being over 180 feet long.

FROCESTER HILL

(1—NE) (3 miles South of Stonehouse)
A lovely open place on the Cotswold edge, with
splendid views out over the Severn estuary. Gliders
from the nearby club add further colour and interest.

HETTY PEGLER'S TUMP

(See **Uley Tumulus,** Page 37)

KINGSCOTE

(1—SE) (4 miles East of Dursley)
Agreeable village in high country, with an over-restored
13th century church. This has a Perpendicular tower
and several interesting monuments in the churchyard.
Here, in 1788, Catherine Kingscote was married to
Doctor Edward Jenner, the discoverer of vaccination...
a marriage which 'brought him much happiness'.

KING'S STANLEY

(1—NE) (1 mile South of Stonehouse)
Lies beneath the Cotswold edge and is rather overpow-
ered by modern development. However it has a
pleasant centre, with several interesting old buildings,
mostly in timber or brick. At the north end of the
village there is a partly Norman church lying in a long
churchyard with clipped yews. Do not miss the grave-
stone of bar-maid, Ann Collins (1804), with copper
plaque inscribed:

> 'Twas as she tript from cask to cask
> In at a bung hole quickly fell
> Suffocation was her task
> She had not time to say farewell.'

LEONARD STANLEY

(1—NE) (1 mile South of Stonehouse)
Its fine monastic church (fragmentary remains of
priory in farm buildings) looks out over a small green
with a few brick and stone cottages, and beside it there
is a lovely 18th century fronted farmhouse. The cruciform church has a beautiful interior with four Norman
arches at the tower crossing, exquisitely carved capitals
to the chancel vaulting shafts and many other interesting features.

NORTH NIBLEY

(1—SW) (2 miles South West of Dursley)
Situated in the very shadow of the Tyndale Monument
(P 9), this small village is thought to have been
Tyndale's birthplace. The largely Perpendicular church
lies to the west of the village and has an unusually
attractive 19th century chancel (designed by J.L. Pearson, the architect of Truro Cathedral).

MAP 1   8

NYMPSFIELD

(1—SE) (4 miles North East of Dursley)

Moderately attractive village sheltering just behind the high Cotswold edge, with a pleasant inn, the Rose and Crown, and a 19th century church. This has a Perpendicular tower complete with gargoyles, turret stair and a handsome clock face.

The nearby Nympsfield Long Barrow (See Map) is open to the sky, and provides a good opportunity to see the layout of a typical Cotswold Long Barrow. This can best be visited from the nearby Coaley Peak Picnic Site.

The Rose & Crown, Nympsfield

OWLPEN

(1—SE) (3 miles East of Dursley)

An exquisite group of buildings in a deep hollow beneath woodlands. There is a fine 15th century manor house (with 16th, 17th and 18th century alterations and additions), a small Victorian church above it, and a little 18th century mill not far away. All this is framed by clipped yews, and backed by steep woods above... a perfect example of a small Cotswold estate.

THE WILDFOWL TRUST, SLIMBRIDGE

(To the immediate West of Map 1)

Situated just off our map, one mile to the north west of Slimbridge (stop to look at the fine 12th and 13th century church), this is the largest and most varied collection of waterfowl in the world. Go in winter if you wish to see wild geese on the shores of the estuary from observation towers.

Church and Manor, Owlpen

STINCHCOMBE HILL

(1—SW) (1 mile North West of Dursley)

Part of this area is used as a golf course, but there is parking space for cars, good walking opportunities and fine views out over the Berkeley Vale, especially from Drakestone Point.

STONEHOUSE

(1—NE) (3 miles West of Stroud)

A largely industrial town, with a church re-built by the Victorians. This in itself is not of great interest, but it is pleasantly situated, looking across a meadow to a pretty stretch of the Stroudwater Canal, and the hills beyond. Elizabethan Stonehouse Court overlooks the churchyard.

Owlpen Manor

STROUDWATER CANAL

(1—NE)

This ran from Framilode, on the Severn below Gloucester, to Stroud, where it linked with the Thames and Severn Canal (P 31). Unhappily it closed in 1927, but brave attempts are being made to restore certain sections, both of this and the Thames and Severn Canal.

THE TYNDALE MONUMENT

(1—SW) (2 miles South West of Dursley)

Ask for key in North Nibley, and walk steeply up from the village, to this 111 feet high tower, built in 1866, in memory of William Tyndale, the translator of the Bible into English (born 1484). Fine views of the Severn estuary from the top.

ULEY   see P 37.

ULEY TUMULUS   see P 37.

Stroudwater Canal, near Stonehouse

MAP 1

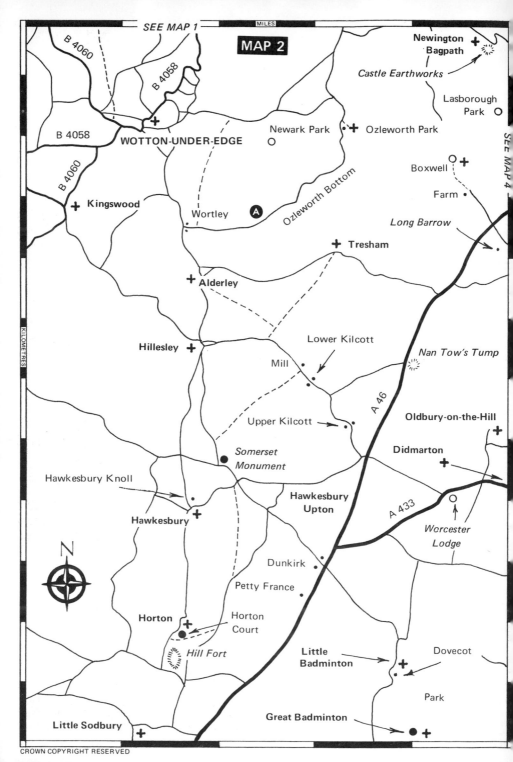

MILES

MAP 2

SEE MAP 1

B 4060

B 4058

B 4058

B 4060

Newington Bagpath

Castle Earthworks

Lasborough Park

WOTTON-UNDER-EDGE

Newark Park

Ozleworth Park

Boxwell

Farm

Kingswood

Wortley

Ⓐ

Ozleworth Bottom

Long Barrow

Tresham

Alderley

Hillesley

Lower Kilcott

Nan Tow's Tump

Mill

Upper Kilcott

A 46

Oldbury-on-the-Hill

Somerset Monument

Didmarton

Hawkesbury Knoll

Hawkesbury

Hawkesbury Upton

A 433

Worcester Lodge

N

Dunkirk

Petty France

Horton

Horton Court

Hill Fort

Little Badminton

Dovecot

Park

Little Sodbury

Great Badminton

KILOMETRES

SEE MAP 4

Map 2

The Far South West

ALDERLEY, BADMINTON, HORTON COURT, WOOTTON-UNDER-EDGE, etc. . . .

ALDERLEY

(2—NW) (2 miles South East of Wotton-under-Edge) Rosehill, next to the church, was built by the industrious Vulliamy in 1860, but there are several earlier houses in this small village. The church, apart from its Perpendicular tower, was re-built in 1802, and has an elegant white painted interior, with a series of stylish monuments, one by the celebrated Sir Francis Chantrey.

BOXWELL

(2—NE) (4 miles East of Wotton-under-Edge) This is not signed from the A 46, but it is possible to drive as far as Boxwell Farm, and then walk straight ahead for about half a mile along a track marked (with ample justification) "UNSUITABLE FOR MOTOR VEHICLES". Here, in a quiet and beautiful valley, you will find a small 13th century church full of character, which is complete with a most unusual stone bellcote, topped with a miniature spire. The church lies beside Boxwell court, which looks Victorian at first sight, but which actually dates from the 15th century

DIDMARTON

(2—SE just off map) (6 miles South West of Tetbury) Handsome stone village astride the busy A 433, with an unexceptional Victorian church, and a fascinating, but rather neglected medieval church. This has a completely unspoilt 18th century interior with fine three decker pulpit, and high backed pews. We hope that efforts will be made to save these treasures from further decay.

GREAT BADMINTON and BADMINTON HOUSE

(2—SE just off map) (9 miles South West of Tetbury) Delightful estate village with houses and cottages of the 17th, 18th and 19th centuries. The church, built in 1785, is attached to the mansion, and contains a splendid series of monuments to the Dukes of Beaufort. Badminton House dates from the latter half of the 17th century, when the Somerset family had to abandon Raglan Castle. (The Third Marquess was created the First Duke of Beaufort in 1682.) William Kent embellished it in the 18th century and built the lovely Worcester Lodge at the north end of the park (view from A 433, west of Didmarton). The game of badminton was invented here, the standard measurements being dictated by the dimensions of its hall. However, Badminton is now best known for the horse trials, held in its magnificent park each spring.

In Alderley Churchyard

Badminton House

Lodge at Badminton

Hawkesbury Church

The Portcullis Inn, Hillesley

Horton Court

Lower Kilcott Mill

HAWKESBURY

(2–SW) (4 miles South of Wotton-under-Edge) The tall towered, mainly Perpendicular church stands almost alone, where a wooded valley opens out from the hilly edge. It all looks splendid from the outside, but once through the Norman north doorway, one is greeted with a brutally scraped interior. However, stop to look at the 15th century stone pulpit and the monuments to the Jenkinson family (one of whom, the Second Earl of Liverpool, was Prime Minister at the time of Waterloo).

HAWKESBURY UPTON

(2–SE) (4 miles South East of Wotton-under-Edge) A bleak, rather indeterminate village, with two inns named the Duke of Beaufort, and, rather appropriately the Fox.

HILLESLEY (or HILLSLEY)

(2–NW) (2½ miles South of Wotton-under-Edge) Modest village endowed with a severe little Bapist chapel, two inns, the Portcullis and the Fleece, and an ambitious Victorian church.

HORTON and HORTON COURT

(2–SW) (5 miles South of Wotton-under-Edge) Lies beneath an Iron Age promontory fort, with its church about half a mile beyond. This is set beneath the wooded Cotswold edge, beside Horton Court, a lovely manor house, with a Norman hall and a detached 16th century ambulatory. The church has a well proportioned Perpendicular tower and a vaulted porch of the same period. In the pleasantly white painted interior there is a Jacobean pulpit, and two handsome 18th century wall tablets.

KINGSWOOD

(2–NW) (1 mile South West of Wotton-under-Edge) Has an early 18th century church, which was over-restored, and partly re-built in 1900. All that survives of the great Cistercian abbey of Kingswood is the 16th century gatehouse, which was completed only a few years before the rest was destroyed (Dissolution of the monasteries 1539), and which is therefore one of the 'youngest' examples of monastic building in the country'.

LITTLE SODBURY

(2–SW) (2 miles North East of Chipping Sodbury) The fine medieval manor house where William Tyndale (P 9) was almost certainly tutor in 1522–3, is' just south of our map area. The unexceptional Victorian church is claimed to be based upon the plans of 'Tyndales chapel' behind the manor house, and the handsome Victorian pulpit has a carved figure of Tyndale upon it.

LOWER KILCOTT

(2–NE) (3½ miles South East of Wotton-under-Edge) Quiet little hamlet tucked away in the edge country, with a small 18th century water mill, with some of its machinery still intact. (NOT OPEN TO THE PUBLIC.)

MAP 2   12

NEWINGTON BAGPATH

(2—NE) (4 miles East of Wotton-under-Edge)
Minute hamlet in a quiet valley overlooked by the circular earthworks (or motte) of a medieval castle, and a small church beside it. We found the church locked but still enjoyed our visit to the tranquil, overgrown churchyard, with its views out over the valley. The squat tower has an attractively hipped roof, and through the windows we could see a Jacobean pulpit. Apart from this there are old choir stalls and reredos, but little else of interest appears to have survived the restorations of 1858.

OLDBURY-ON-THE-HILL

(2—SE) (6 miles South West of Tetbury)
A hamlet to the immediate north of Didmarton, with a small church beside an extensive farm, and the Beaufort Hunt point-to-point course close by. Within the white painted interior of the church are high backed pews, and an 18th century two-decker pulpit.

OZLEWORTH

(2—NE) (2½ miles East of Wotton-under-Edge)
Walk up the short drive to handsome 18th century Ozleworth Park and round behind it to visit the Norman church. This has a very rare hexagonal tower, and stands in a circular churchyard. Well worth the walk.

PETTY FRANCE

(2—SE) (8 miles South West of Tetbury)
Hamlet astride the busy A 46, with an agreeable hotel. Its name was probably derived from Westminster's Petty France.

SOMERSET MONUMENT, THE

(2—SW) (3½ miles South of Wotton-under-Edge)
High stone tower with a slightly oriental flavour, built by Lewis Vulliamy in 1846, and commemorating General Lord Robert Somerset. At least six counties may be seen from the top of this formidable landmark.

TRESHAM

(2—NE) (3 miles South East of Wotton-under-Edge)
This is a small, rather scrappy village.....but it is gloriously situated, with views south westwards along the hilly edge to the Somerset Monument. The little neo-Norman church is very severe outside, but some of the sculptural details inside are rather pleasing.

UPPER KILCOTT

(2—SE) (4 miles South East of Wotton-under-Edge)
Tidy little hamlet near the head of a deep wooded valley running up into the Cotswold edge.

WOTTON-UNDER-EDGE

(2—NW) (3 miles South of Dursley)
Attractive little town which still shows signs of its prosperity in the 17th and 18th century cloth trade. The church has a fine Perpendicular tower and a large over restored interior. Do not miss the splendid late 14th century brasses of Lord and Lady Berkeley (glass fibre copy usually on display).

WORTLEY

(2—NW) (1 mile South of Wotton-under-Edge)
Minute hamlet at the foot of Ozleworth Bottom.

Newington Bagpath Church

In Ozleworth Bottom — Map Ref. ⒶA

The Somerset Monument

In Wotton-under-Edge

South Porch. Wotton-under-Edge

MAP 2

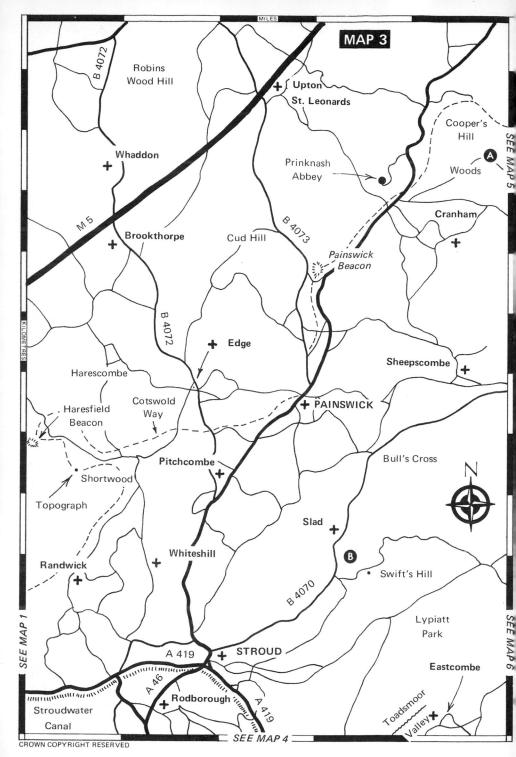

MILES

MAP 3

B 4072

Robins
Wood Hill

Upton
St. Leonards

Cooper's
Hill

Whaddon

Prinknash
Abbey

Woods

A

M 5

Cranham

Brookthorpe

Cud Hill

B 4073

Painswick
Beacon

B 4072

Edge

Sheepscombe

Harescombe

Cotswold
Way

Haresfield
Beacon

PAINSWICK

Shortwood

Pitchcombe

Bull's Cross

Topograph

N

Slad

Whiteshill

B

Randwick

Swift's Hill

B 4070

Lypiatt
Park

A 419

STROUD

Eastcombe

A 46

Rodborough

A 419

Stroudwater
Canal

Toadsmoor
Valley

SEE MAP 4

SEE MAP 5

SEE MAP 6

SEE MAP 1

KILOMETRES

Map 3

Cloth Valleys and Western Beacons

PAINSWICK, PRINKNASH ABBEY, SLAD, STROUD, etc....

ROOKTHORPE

(3—NW) (5 miles North of Stroud)
minute scatter of a village sandwiched between the
otswold edge and the noisy M 5 motorway. The 13th
entury church has a saddle-back tower, and on one of
he north arcade pillars, are carved the names of the
arishoners who died in the first war.....an unusual and
leasing way of recording their sacrifice. Beside the
hurch stands Brookthorpe Court, a partly 17th cent-
ry building in timber and stone, emphasising this
illage's position between hill and valley country.

COOPER'S HILL

(3–NE) (7 miles North East of Stroud)
he well known Cheese Rolling competition takes
lace here every Whit Monday. There is a small car
ark in Cooper's Hill hamlet (half a mile to the east of
he A 46), and from here a 'Nature Trail' leads to the
op of the hill, with its Maypole at the head of the
heese rolling slope. This lies on the Cotswold Way (P 5)
nd one can also walk south east from the car park to
/itcombe Roman Villa (P 27).

RANHAM

(3—NE) (6 miles North East of Stroud)
cattered village lying near the head of the Painswick
alley, with an extensive common to the south east,
nd great beech woodlands to the north. There is a
riendly little inn called the Black Horse, but also
ather too many 'between the wars' bungalows for our
king. The largely 15th century church stands high up,
rell to the south of the village, with fine views down
he valley. See especially the sheep shears carved on the
econd stage of the tower, the early 16th century rood
creen, the beautiful 'triptych' reredos, and the hand-
ome monument to Obadiah Done (1758) 'Rector of
his parish 57 years'.

ASTCOMBE

(3–SE) (2½ miles East of Stroud)
spread out on a hillside overlooking the Toadsmoor
alley, with considerable modern development, and
ttle of interest for the visitor apart from the snug
amb Inn.

DGE

(3–SW) (3 miles North of Stroud)
mall village with views westwards over the Severn
alley, and eastwards to Painswick. Its modest Victor-
n church has a neat little stone spire, but is otherwise
nexceptional.

In Buckholt Wood, near Cranham — Map Ref Ⓐ

Bull's Cross, near Painswick

Blossom Time at Edge

The Cross, Painswick

Sunshine at Painswick

Painswick Church

Painswick Beacon

The Old Abbey, Prinknash

HARESFIELD BEACON

(3—SW) (3 miles North West of Strouc
There is a topograph, or viewing table, in the Shor
wood area, and beyond this, car parking space for thos
who wish to walk along to the beacon itself, a hill to
surmounted by an Iron Age promontory fort. Splendi
views from both points.

PAINSWICK

(3—SE) (3 miles North of Strouc
Situated on a high spur between two valleys, Pains
wick is an elegant town, made prosperous by the cloth
ing industry in the 17th and 18th centuries. Bisley
much quieter, but here we have a more sophisticate
scene.....the church with its fine 17th century spire, it
famous clipped yews, and splendid series of tabl
tombs.....all this surrounded by houses, shops, hotel
and inns, almost all in light grey stone, and many o
which are embellished with small architectural details
bringing further pleasure to the eye. All we have to d
is dispose of the A 46, and we would have perfectior

PITCHCOMBE

(3—SW) (2 miles North of Strouc
Attractive hillside village with lovely Pitchcombe Hous
standing close to a terrace of older houses lookin
southwards. The church was entirely re-built in the 19t
century, and is a dignified if rather dull building
relieved only by the handsome table tombs an
clipped yews in the churchyard; both no doub
inspired by Pitchcombe's proximity to Painswick

PAINSWICK BEACON

(3—NE) (1½ miles North of Painswick
Attractive open country with pine trees, old quarrie
and a golf course nearby. If you value tranqullity avoi
Sunday afternoons.

PRINKNASH ABBEY

(3—NE) (2½ miles North East of Painswick
Its establishment dates from 1928, when a Benedictin
community moved here from Caldey Island. Howeve
the 'old abbey', which shelters below wooded hillside
with views out over the Severn plain, was built here i
the 14th century, as a grange of the Abbots of Glouce
ster. The new monastic building is now complete, an
visitors are encouraged to look round the potter
There is also an attractive Bird Garden in part of th
abbey grounds.

RANDWICK

(3—SW) (1½ miles North West of Strouc
Its lower parts are now more a suburb of Stroud, bu
the rest is full of character. It is attractively sited c
steep hillsides beneath Standish Wood, with an in
called the Vine Tree, and a Victorian church (wit
Perpendicular tower) sitting below the road in a shad
sloping churchyard. The Cotswold Way (P 5) ru
through Standish Wood.

RODBOROUGH

(3—SW) (1 mile South West of Strou
Now a hilly suburb of Stroud, it has a Victorian churc
which like so many others, has retained a Perpendicul
tower. (For Rodborugh Common, see P 21).

MAP 3　　　　16

SHEEPSCOMBE

(3—NE) (1½ miles East of Painswick)
Beautifully situated, on both sides of a quiet valley, beneath luxuriously wooded hillsides. The Butcher's Arms has a colourful carved sign, and across the valley, immediately above a sloping green, there is a quaint little Victorian church, with a minute tower at its ornate west end.

SLAD

(3—SE) (2 miles North East of Stroud)
This small village, strung out along the B 4010, is inevitably linked with poet and author, Laurie Lee, who has so richly endowed us with the memories of childhood days at Slad, in his brilliant book, 'Cider with Rosie'.

The Star Inn, Slad

STROUD

(3—SW) (8 miles South of Gloucester)
Built on the steep slopes of the Frome (or Golden) Valley, Stroud has retained considerable character despite its industrialisation in the late 18th and early 19th centuries. It had in fact established itself as the pre-eminent centre of the Cotswold cloth industry as early as the 15th century, and the availability of Cotswold wool, of water for washing, and of minerals for dyeing and cleaning, ensured that it remained so for several hundred years. High quality cloth is still produced here, but only in about six mills. However various industries have come here to replace cloth, and Stroud and its surrounding valley country is still bustling with activity. Visitors should concentrate on the Parish Church, a Victorian building with several earlier monuments, and a fine 14th century tower; and the interesting little Stroud Museum, which tells the story of Stroud's achievements as a cloth and industrial centre.

Laurie Lee Country, Slad — Map Ref **B**

SWIFTS HILL

(3—SE) (2 miles North East of Stroud)
This is a Nature Reserve and is a pleasantly scrubby, grass covered area, which should be left undisturbed as much as possible. There is an attractive road from Slad over to Bisley, passing Swifts Hill, with mouth watering views back over to Slad.

TOADSMOOR VALLEY

(3—SE) (2 miles East of Stroud)
Deep wooded valley running up from Brimscombe (P 20) almost to Bisley (P 29), but mostly situated on this map. Old cloth mills now used for light industry.

Stratford Park, Stroud

UPTON ST. LEONARDS

(3—NE) (3 miles North of Painswick)
Scattered village below Prinknash Abbey, with timber framed farms and cottages now greatly outnumbered by modern houses. Gloucester is not far away, and the noisy M 5 motorway is depressingly close to the church. This has a handsome Perpendicular tower, but otherwise owes too much to the Victorians. However do not miss the fine monument to Sir Thomas Snell in the north chapel.

WHADDON see P 41.

WHITESHILL see P 41.

Swifts Hill

MAP 3

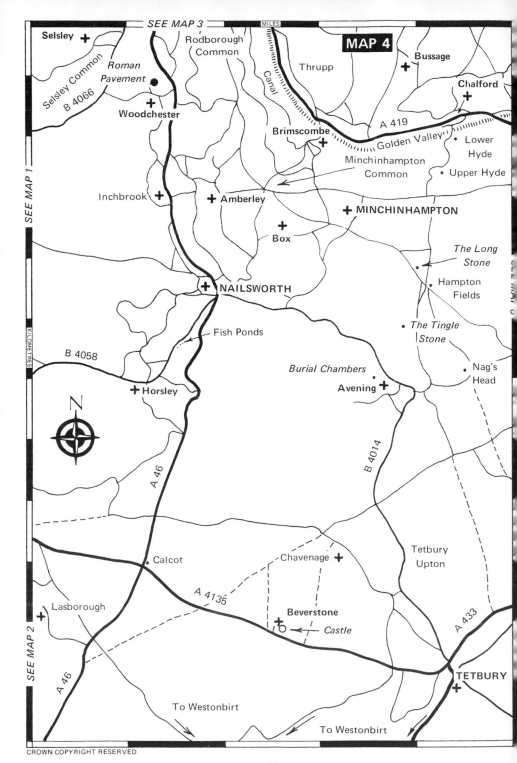

18

Map 4

Deep Valleys and Broad Uplands

AMBERLEY, CHALFORD, MINCHINHAMPTON, TETBURY, WESTONBIRT, etc. . . .

AMBERLEY

(4—NW) (1 mile North of Nailsworth)
A scattered village on the high edge of Minchinhampton Common, with splendid views westwards out over the Avon valley. Much of the novel John Halifax Gentleman was centred here....Mrs. Craik, its authoress lived at Rose Cottage.

AVENING

(4—SE) (2 miles South East of Nailsworth)
Large village near the head of the Avon valley, with pleasant old shops, houses and inns. The handsome early Norman church is well sited in a steep sloping churchyard, and has an interesting interior including a small 'museum' in the south transept. Situated about a quarter of a mile to the north of the church are three interesting burial chambers, one with a rare 'porthole' entrance. All three came from a long barrow near Nag's Head.

In Avening Churchyard

BEVERSTONE

(4—SE) (2 miles West of Tetbury)
Small village on the A 4135, with several cottages built by Vulliamy for the Holfords, who purchased the Beverstone estate in 1842 (see Westonbirt P 51). Here is one of the few surviving Cotswold castles.....a 13th century building with 17th century domestic additions and alterations. It is not open to the public, but glimpses may be obtained from the main road, and from the little roadway up to the church. The latter has an interesting Anglo-Saxon sculpture of the Resurrection on the south face of its tower. The pleasant white washed interior reveals several signs of Vulliamy's restoration of 1844 (e.g. nave roof), but we especially liked the original parts of the 15th century rood screen and the details in the south arcade capitals. Do not miss a glimpse of the lovely 18th century rectory on the opposite side of the church driveway to the castle.

Beverstone Rectory

BOX

(4—NW) (½ mile North East of Nailsworth)
Small village on a steep hillside below Minchinhampton Common, with a little church built as recently as 1953, and some pleasant views down into the Avon valley

Beverstone Castle

19

MAP 4

Chavenage

The Long Stone, near Hampton Fields

Round House at Hyde

On Minchinhampton Common

BRIMSCOMBE

(4—NE) (1 mile North of Minchinhampton
A rather scrappy village in the deep Golden Valley
with a Victorian church on the hillside above. Brims
combe 'port' was the headquarters of the Thames and
Severn Canal, and several pleasant old buildings by
the canal still bear witness to the architectural harmony
of the early Industrial Revolution. Weeping willow
and mellow brick enhance this atmosphere despite the
presence of a foundry and other industrial works

BUSSAGE

(4—NE) (2½ miles South East of Stroud
Small village on high slopes above the wooded Toads
moor Valley, with a beautifully sited little Victorian
church and a character inn called the Ram.

CHALFORD

(4—NE) (3 miles South East of Stroud
A fascinating, large village, built in terraces on the steep
northern slopes of the Golden Valley, with a wealth of
pleasant late 18th and early 19th century houses, most
of which once belonged to clothiers, and many delight
ful cottages, once inhabited by weavers. In the valley
there are old mills on the banks of the now derelic
Thames and Severn Canal, and on the main road, a
rather severe 18th century church. PLEASE EXPLORE
CHALFORD ON FOOT.

CHAVENAGE

(4—SE) (1½ miles North West of Tetbury
A delicious 16th century manor house is visible from
the road. It is also possible to walk behind it to the
little church, but this is not of great interest apar
from some 17th century tomb figures which have
been re-set in the porch.

HAMPTON FIELDS

(4—NE) (1 mile South East of Minchinhampton
Hamlet with a pleasant row of 18th and early 19th
century cottages. The Long Stone, the only surviving
stone from a vanished long barrow, stands in a field to
the east of the road from here to Minchinhampton

HORSLEY

(4—NW) (1 mile South West of Nailsworth
An unexceptional village situated in high country on
the busy B 4058 (note the fish breeding ponds in the
valley between here and Nailsworth). Its priory ha
long since vanished, and the only remains of the
medieval church is the tower. The rest of this rathe
impressive church was designed in 1838 by Thomas
Rickman, who is better known as the original classifier
of the styles of English architecture.....'Early English'
'Decorated' and 'Perpendicular'.

HYDE, UPPER and LOWER

(4—NE) (1½ miles North East of Minchinhampton
Upper Hyde hamlet overlooks the Golden Valley, and
Lower Hyde, in the valley itself, has a fine 'Round
House', built beside the Thames and Severn Canal,
restored fragment of which exists here. These 'Round
Houses' several of which we shall encounter, were
built for the canal maintenance men (known in the
canal world as 'length men').

MAP 4   20

LASBOROUGH

(4—SW) (4 miles South West of Nailsworth)
A 17th century manor house and a small Victorian church overlook a quiet valley in which lies an 18th century mansion built by James Wyatt (Lasborough Park). A drive or walk, as far as the church, makes a pleasant diversion from the busy A 46.

MINCHINHAMPTON

(4—NE) (1½ miles North East of Nailsworth)
Situated high up on the eastern fringes of Minchinhampton Common (580 glorious acres), this is one of our favourite Cotswold cloth towns. See especially the 18th century Crown Hotel, and the fascinating Market House. The church has a fine 14th century south transept and an unusually truncated spire. Do not miss the vaulting beneath the tower, nor the interesting brasses.

Minchinhampton

NAG'S HEAD

(4—NE) (3 miles East of Nailsworth)
Delicious little hamlet taking its name from an inn of that name, now a private house. It has a row of small houses looking southwards over a quiet valley..... everyone's dream for retirement.

NAILSWORTH

(4—NW) (4 miles South of Stroud)
Superficially this is one of the less attractive Cotswold cloth towns and appears to be much dominated by its unattractive centre and the busy A 46 which cuts through it. However on the slopes above the valley bottom are a multitude of attractive streets and alleyways, which will amply re-pay those who explore on foot. See especially the 17th century Quaker Meeting House.

Nag's Head

RODBOROUGH COMMON

(4—NW) (2½ miles North of Nailsworth)
Pleasant open common land on high ground between the Avon Valley and the Golden Valley. Rodborough Fort, a turreted Victorian house, has a well run caravan site beside it.....a good centre for touring the southern Cotswolds.

SELSLEY and SELSLEY COMMON

(4—NW) (2 miles South West of Stroud)
Hillside village with an interesting Victorian church, which contains glass by almost all the Pre-Raphaelites. There is also a splendid open stretch of common land.

On Rodborough Common

TETBURY

(4—SE) (5 miles South East of Nailsworth)
Small market town, and antiques centre, on the busy A 433. Its 17th century Market House, on three rows of delightfully dumpy pillars, was used for wool trading and there are many handsome 17th and 18th century houses in Tetbury that bear witness to its prosperity as a wool collecting centre for the cloth towns and villages to its north and west. The elegant 18th century Gothic church, with its beautifully proportioned interior should on no account be missed.

WESTONBIRT ARBORETUM see P 51

WOODCHESTER see P 51

WOODCHESTER ROMAN PAVEMENT see P 51

Market House, Tetbury

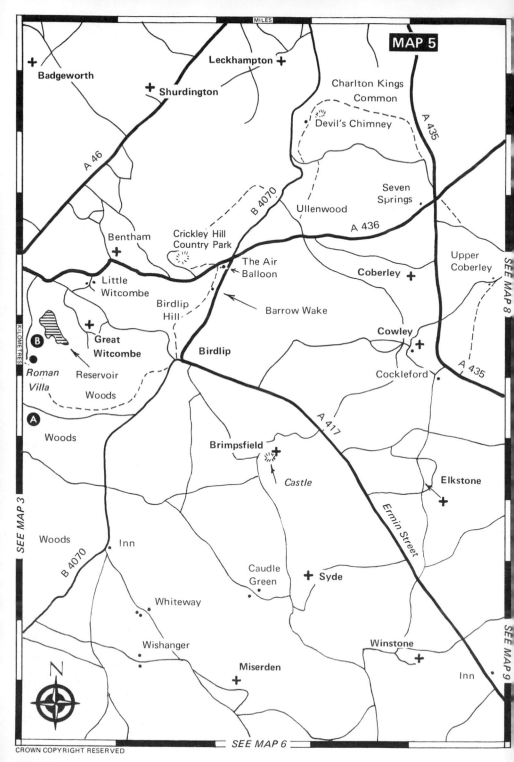

MAP 5

Badgeworth

Leckhampton

Shurdington

Charlton Kings Common

Devil's Chimney

A 435

A 46

B 4070

Seven Springs

Ullenwood

A 436

Bentham

Crickley Hill Country Park

The Air Balloon

Coberley

Upper Coberley

Little Witcombe

Birdlip Hill

Barrow Wake

Great Witcombe

Birdlip

Cowley

Roman Villa

Reservoir

Woods

Cockleford

A 435

A 417

Woods

Brimpsfield

Castle

Elkstone

Ermin Street

Woods

Inn

B 4070

Caudle Green

Syde

Whiteway

Wishanger

Winstone

Miserden

Inn

N

SEE MAP 8

SEE MAP 3

SEE MAP 9

KILOMETRES

MILES

SEE MAP 6

22

Map 5

Western Slopes and a Southern River

BIRDLIP, DEVIL'S CHIMNEY, SEVEN SPRINGS, WITCOMBE ROMAN VILLA, etc. . . .

BADGEWORTH

(5—NW) (3 miles South West of Cheltenham)
A small surprisingly quiet village between heavily populated Cheltenham and Gloucester, with its church tucked away at the end of a short cul-de-sac. The large churchyard is approached through an attractively carved lych gate, and beyond lies the base of an old cross, and several pleasant 18th and 19th century tombs (see especially those to Henry and William Bubb). The church has a well proportioned Perpendicular tower, and a beautiful 14th century north aisle chapel....regarded as the finest specimen of the Decorated period in Gloucestershire, with elaborate ball-flower ornamentation to door and windows. Do not miss the splendid roof to the chapel, with its lovely angel corbel figures.

Badgeworth Church   In Badgeworth Churchyard

BARROW WAKE

(5—NW) (4 miles South of Cheltenham)
This is a fine viewpoint on the Cotswold edge, on the A 417, just south of the Air Balloon Inn; complete with good parking facilities beside the road, and an unusual stone indicator illustrating the geology of the area. It was in this area that the famous Birdlip Mirror was discovered. This outstanding example of Celtic (Iron Age) art, is to be seen in Gloucester Museum.

Barrow Wake

BENTHAM

(5—NW) (4 miles South West of Cheltenham)
Widespread hamlet below the Cotswold edge at Crickley Hill, with an unexceptional Victorian church on the A 417.

BIRDLIP

(5—NW) (5 miles South of Cheltenham)
Small village marking the end of the Ermin Street's steep climb up from the Severn plain. Great beech woods clothe the steep Cotswold edge and the atmosphere of a welcome coaching stop still lingers. There is a small church, built here as recently as 1957 to replace a Victorian one destroyed by fire.

BRIMPSFIELD

(5—SW) (6 miles South of Cheltenham)
The manor of Brimpsfield was given by William the Conqueror to the Giffard family, who built two castles here.....a wooden one on a mound over towards Ermin Street, and later on, a large stone building close to the church. However in 1322 John Giffard was foolish

Brimpsfield Church

MAP 5

At Caudle Green

Cowley Manor Gardens

The Green Dragon, Cockleford

In Cranham Wood — Map Ref. Ⓐ

enough to cross Edward II's path and he was hanged at Gloucester and the castle demolished. This was never re-built, but its earthworks are still visible in trees to the right of a path to the church. This is situated on the edge of the village in a large churchyard with many 18th century tombstones. It has a 15th century tower which 'descends' into the centre of the building, providing us with a fascinating architectural puzzle. Do not overlook the scanty remains of the 12th century priory in the walls of an old barn over to the left of the churchyard as we enter.

CAUDLE GREEN

(5—SE) (7 miles North West of Cirencester)
A hillside hamlet looking across a deep wooded valley to Syde, with a rough green overlooked by a pleasant 18th century farmhouse.

COBERLEY

(5—NE) (4 miles South of Cheltenham)
Small village delightfully situated near the head of the Churn valley (less than a mile below its source at Seven Springs.....P 26). The church lies a little way to the east of the village and is approached by a path beneath an archway in a farm building (one feels that one is intruding, but there is no alternative). Most of the church was re-built in the 19th century, but the Perpendicular tower and the 14th century south chapel have survived. This chapel contains the effigies of Sir Thomas Berkeley, who fought at Crecy, and his wife Joan, who re-married after Sir Thomas's death and became the mother of Sir Richard (Dick) Whittington. In the sanctuary there is a monument of a knight holding a heart, commemorating the burial of Sir Giles Berkeley's heart here in 1295 (his body was buried at Little Malvern).

The high walls by the churchyard and the large flat area beyond are the only surviving evidence of a mansion that stood here until the 18th century.

COCKLEFORD

(5—NE) (5 miles South of Cheltenham)
Hamlet blessed with an inn serving really good bread and cheese and excellent beer...the Green Dragon... an excellent place, happily remembered.

COWLEY

(5—NE) (4½ miles South of Cheltenham)
Cowley Manor a 19th century Italianate mansion in exquisite gardens with lake and ornamental ponds, is now used by Gloucestershire County Council for various educational activities. The church, lying beside the manor, is not very interesting.

CRANHAM WOOD

(5—SW) (6 miles South of Cheltenham)
This is part of a glorious area of woodland between Birdlip and Prinknash Abbey, with beech trees predominating. Parking facilities are limited, but for best access drive south west from Birdlip on B 4070 and fork right after one mile.....Cranham Wood to left..... Witcombe Wood to right. The other good access point is in the vicinity of Cranham village (P 15).

MAP 5   24

CRICKLEY HILL COUNTRY PARK

(5—NW) (4 miles South of Cheltenham)
Thirty acres of Cotswold edge country owned by the National Trust, with fine views out over the Severn valley; part of an Iron Age promontory fort, and nearby, the Devil's Table, an attractive rocky outcrop (but less dramatic than the Devil's Chimney).

The Devil's Chimney

DEVIL'S CHIMNEY, THE

(5—NE) (2 miles South of Cheltenham)
Dramatic limestone outcrop detached from the Cotswold edge, with splendid views out over Cheltenham to the Malvern Hills. Drive south from Cheltenham on B 4070 for about two miles.....fork left up a steep road towards Salterley Grange Sanatorium. Park as soon as possible, and walk up left, and along a beautiful hillside terrace for about a quarter of a mile. The area near the chimney has been extensively quarried and great|care|should be|exercised. There is a small Iron Age hill fort on the hill above.

Our path is part of the Cotswold Way (P 5) and from the Devil's Chimney one can walk on eastwards along Charlton Kings Common, and then south to Seven Springs (P 26).

ELKSTONE

(5—SE) (6 miles South of Cheltenham)
Small village with a handsome 18th century rectory and an outstandingly interesting Norman church. There is a Norman south doorway, with tympanum and beak heads, and a beautiful little stone vaulted Norman chancel. See also the fine Perpendicular tower, the box pews, and the 17th century table tombs near the south porch. DON'T MISS THIS.

Elkstone Church

ERMIN STREET

(Maps 5—9 13)
A Roman road stretching from Silchester (near Reading), through Cricklade and Cirencester, to the legionary fortress at Gloucester. Modern roads still follow the Ermin Street across the Cotswolds.....the A 419 as far as Cirencester, and the A 417 northwards to Gloucester. Beware, when turning on to Ermin Street.....traffic makes all too good a use of the Roman straightness, and travels depressingly fast.....a rather doubtful heritage from the past.

FIVE MILE HOUSE

(5—SE) (5 miles North West of Cirencester)
Pleasant stone built inn, on the Ermin Street, about a mile to the north east of Duntisbourne Abbots (P 30).

Table Tomb at Elkstone

FOSTON'S ASH INN

(5—SW) (6 miles South East of Gloucester)
Hospitable inn on the B 4070, about two miles south of Birdlip.

GREAT WITCOMBE

(5—NW) (5 miles South West of Cheltenham)
Quiet village tucked away beneath the wooded Cotswold edge at Birdlip, with hills on three sides and a reservoir just below. Here are a few half-timbered cottages, a dignified little 19th century school and school house, and a fascinating church. A massive yew tree is close to the attractive 18th century porch, which is contemporary with the handsome tower. However the interior is even more pleasing, with Norman chancel arch, a barrel vaulted ceiling to the nave (? also 18th

Great Witcombe Church

MAP 5

At Miserden

Monument at Miserden

Seven Springs

From Shurdington Porch

Syde Church

century), a medieval rood beam, and fragments of medieval glass in the north aisle windows. Do not miss this atmospheric little church.

LECKHAMPTON

(5—NE) (1 mile South of Cheltenham)
Large suburb of Cheltenham, which still retains a flavour of its own at its southern fringes beneath the steep quarries of Leckhampton Hill (see Devil's Chimney, P 25). The church is pleasantly sited, with its slender 14th century tower and spire viewed against a backdrop of hills. Almost all the rest of the church was re-built in the 19th century, but do not miss the fine effigies of Sir John Giffard and his wife (1327), nor the attractive brass of Elizabeth Norwood (1598), with husband, wife, nine sons and two daughters. There is a monument in the churchyard to Edmund Wilson, one of Captain Scott's ill fated companions, on his journey to the South Pole.

MISERDEN

(5—SW) (7 miles North West of Cirencester)
A very trim, largely 19th and 20th century estate village, with small octagonal shelter built around a massive sycamore tree, and overlooked by the hospitable Carpenter's Arms. The church has late Saxon origins and stands in a beautiful churchyard enriched with yew and beech. See especially the elaborately carved and gilded reredos, and the splendid 17th century monuments.

SEVEN SPRINGS

(5—NE) (3 miles South of Cheltenham)
Although this is claimed to be the 'highest source of the Thames', it is in fact the source of its attractive tributary, the Churn (see P 45 for the true source of the Thames). It consists of a rather muddy little pool fed by seven springs, situated between the A 436 and a much used lay-by. Not an enchanted spot!

SHURDINGTON

(5—NW) (3 miles South West of Cheltenham)
Now almost a suburb shared by Cheltenham and Gloucester, its peace is shattered by the busy A 46. However the church lies away from this main road, with yew trees lining the long path to its south porch. This is overlooked by a slender 14th century spire which is even more graceful than its contemporary at nearby Leckhampton. Inside there is fine rib vaulting below the tower, and beneath it, a pleasant 14th century font.....otherwise little of interest to the visitor.

SYDE

(5—SE) (7 miles North West of Cirencester)
Quite hamlet, looking across to Caudle Green, with an early Norman church. This has a small saddle-backed tower and a pleasing 15th century roof, looking more like a barn's than a church's. The chancel is Victorian but even this is pleasant. Do not overlook the 17th century box pews, nor the little 15th century glass roundel in muted colours, of St. James of Compostella. There is a tithe barn on the south side of the churchyard, and the cottage on the right hand side of the road leading down towards Caudle Green has 14th century windows and is believed to be based upon a chantry chapel founded here in 1344 by Sir Thomas Berkeley.

MAP 5

26

ULLENWOOD

(5—NE) (3 miles South of Cheltenham)
Victorian mansion now used as a school.....hence the dramatic new architectural forms visible from the road.

UPPER COBERLEY

(5—NE) (4 miles South East of Cheltenham)
Attractive hamlet overlooking the upper Churn valley, with several open fronted barns.....all supported on stone columns.

WHITEWAY

(5—SW) (6 miles South East of Gloucester)
This 'colony' was founded many years ago by a group of people who wished to follow the ideas set forth by Tolstoy, in the conduct of their own lives. We find it hard to admire the architectural results, but the courage required to re-think a philosophy of life and to follow it through in practical terms, is unquestionable. Let us leave Whiteway undisturbed and move on.....

WINSTONE

(5—SE) (6 miles North West of Cirencester)
A rather indeterminate upland village, with an unusually large number of farms, but nothing of special interest apart from the church. This is pleasantly situated at the very end of the village, looking south and east over open farmland. It has a saddle back tower, but it has been ruthlessly 'restored', both inside and out. The blocked north doorway and the chancel arch with their massive jambs, are Anglo Saxon, but the south doorway is more Norman in feeling. (If one must classify styles at such a shadowy transitional period.) Do not overlook the base and broken shaft of a 14th century cross near the south porch.

WITCOMBE ROMAN VILLA

(5—NW) (4 miles South East of Gloucester)
(Turn south off the A 417 about ¼ mile east of its intersection with A 46 at roundabout, following sign marked Droys Court, after .4 miles bear left at Droys Court, after .7 miles arrive at farm where key to villa may be collected... villa now only a few yards walk beyond.)
This is a 1st century Roman villa, with a small mosaic pavement and various items from the excavation displayed in a small building on the site. It is situated on a terrace beneath high woodlands and there are fine views out over the Severn plain.....a quiet place at the end of a pleasant open road across from the A 417..... proving once again how adept the Romans where at choosing these villa sites.

Barn at Upper Coberley

The Road to Witcombe Roman Villa — Map Ref. ⓑ

Witcombe Roman Villa

Cottage at Syde

At Witcombe Roman Villa

MAP 5

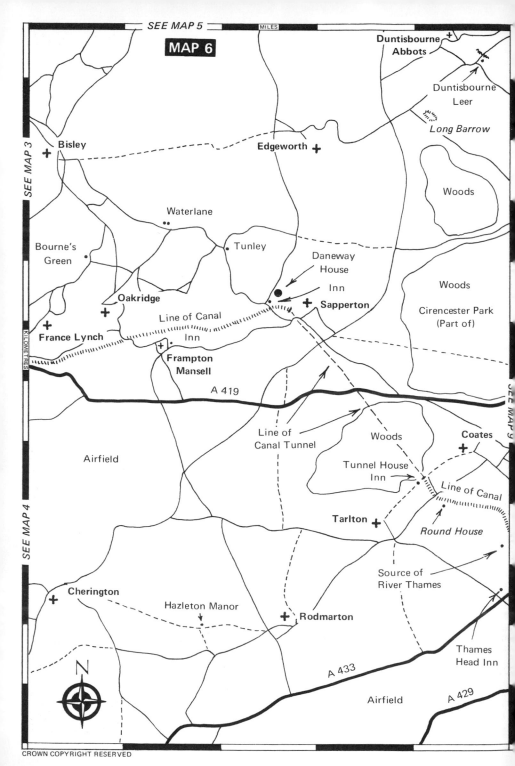

MAP 6

SEE MAP 5

MILES

Duntisbourne Abbots

Duntisbourne Leer

Long Barrow

Bisley

Edgeworth

Woods

Waterlane

Tunley

Daneway House

Inn

Woods

Bourne's Green

Oakridge

Sapperton

Cirencester Park (Part of)

Line of Canal

France Lynch

Inn

Frampton Mansell

A 419

Line of Canal Tunnel

Woods

Coates

Airfield

Tunnel House Inn

Line of Canal

Tarlton

Round House

SEE MAP 3

KILOMETRES

SEE MAP 4

Cherington

Hazleton Manor

Rodmarton

Source of River Thames

Thames Head Inn

A 433

Airfield

A 429

N

28

Map 6

Gentle Valleys, Great Woodlands and an Old Canal

BISLEY, DANEWAY, DUNTISBOURNE ABBOTS, SAPPERTON, etc. . . .

BISLEY

(6—NW) (4 miles East of Stroud)

This large village in upland country well to the north of the Golden Valley is a sheer delight. Everywhere one's eyes roam they are rewarded with good things. The clothiers of the valleys brought their wealth with them to Bisley, and spent wisely.....on splendid houses like Over Court, with its charming 18th century gazebo, handsome Jaynes Court to the south west of the church, and the multitude of more modest, but equally pleasant houses and cottages. The church has a fine spire and a unique 13th century 'Poor Soul's Light' (England's only out door example), but the interior was over zealously restored by the Victorians. However do not overlook the effigy of a 13th century knight, nor the font with its Norman bowl and 19th century stem. Close to the delightful Bear Inn, with its stone support pillars, is a pretty little village lock-up (1824), and below the church is Bisley Wells, a Victorian restoration of seven springs, complete with Gothic details.

Bisley

BOURNE'S GREEN

(6—NW) (4 miles East of Stroud)

Pretty hillside hamlet between Bisley, Oakridge and France Lynch, with steep narrow roads, and pleasant views down a small valley where those clever Romans had a villa (nothing now to be seen).

CHERINGTON

(6—SW) (3½ miles East of Nailsworth)

The unspoilt Yew Tree Inn and several dignified 18th century cottages overlook a large green, which is endowed with a Victorian drinking fountain inscribed 'Let Him that is athirst, come'. The church has a Norman south doorway with tympanum, and an Early English chancel (unfortunately scraped). We particularly liked the pulpit incorporating carved Flemish (?) panels, and the handsome Renaissance candle-holder beside it.

Lock-up at Bisley

Gazebo at Bisley

COATES

(6—SE) (3 miles West of Cirencester)

A small village on the high wolds with a neat Perpendicular towered church, in company with a rectory and farmhouse.....two most beautiful houses. Passing from the tidy churchyard, through a Norman doorway, we were delighted with the simplicity of the church's interior.

Tunnel House Inn Sign, Coates

Round House near Coates

The Daneway Inn..... 'Legger's Haven'

Duntisbourne Abbots

Ford at Duntisbourne Leer

Tombstone at Edgeworth   Incised Tomb Slab,
                          Edgeworth

DANEWAY

(6—NE) (5 miles West of Cirencester)
Here below Sapperton was the north western end of
the Thames and Severn Canal's long tunnel from
Coates (P 29). The Daneway Inn, like the Tunnel
House Inn at the Coates end, must have provided count
less thousands of pints for the thirsty leggers during the
tunnel's short working life between 1789 and 1911

DANEWAY HOUSE

(6—NE) (5 miles West of Cirencester)
A fascinating Manor House dating from the 14th cent
ury, which was used by the Barnsley brothers and
Ernest Gimson (all disciples of William Morris) as furni
ture workshops and showrooms for about twenty years

DUNTISBOURNE ABBOTS

(6—NE) (5 miles North West of Cirencester)
Another very trim village, with widespread evidence of
much time and money being lavished upon its houses
and cottages. The church's chancel has been very
recently restored....white painted and rather pleasant..
but the rest is still 'scraped' and somewhat severe

DUNTISBOURNE LEER

(6—NE) (4½ miles North West of Cirencester)
The unusual name is derived from the Abbey of Lire in
Normandy, to whom this parish originally belonged
Now only a hamlet, Duntisbourne Leer will be remem
bered chiefly for the farmhouse and buildings attrac
tively grouped around the ford.

EDGEWORTH

(6—NE) (5 miles North West of Cirencester)
Has a church and manor house beautifully sited above
the steep wooded slopes of the Frome valley. The inter
ior of the church has been over restored, but don'
miss the 14th century glass (of a bishop) in the chancel

FRAMPTON MANSELL

(6—NW) (6½ miles West of Cirencester)
Small village on the steep southern slopes of the Gold
en Valley, with a handsome neo-Norman church and a
delightful little free-house called the Crown Inn. This i
much restored within, but what excellent bread and
cheese, and what a pleasant prospect from its garden
The only attraction that we miss, is the sound of steam
trains coming up the valley on the old G.W.R. line; but
diesels may still be seen crossing the tall viaduct below
the village, and there are pretty stretches of the old
Thames and Severn Canal in the depths of the valley

FRANCE LYNCH

(6—NW) (3½ miles East of Stroud)
Another steep hillside village, France Lynch is linked
to Chalford (P 20), and has the same delightful flavour
It has a small inn, the King's Head, and an unusually
effective Victorian church. See especially the splendidly
ornate chancel, with its coloured marble inlays and its
three angels playing different musical instruments. The
altar rail kneeling mat, worked by the ladies of the
parish, includes a picture of one of the donkeys which
were used to deliver bread and milk up the steep
village streets.

MAP 6   30

HAZLETON

(6–SW) (4½ miles East of Nailsworth)

There is a fine 16th and 17th century manor house and farmstead, just visible from the road between Rodmarton and Cherington.

OAKRIDGE

(6–NW) (4 miles East of Stroud)

Lies just above the northern slopes of the Golden Valley, with its views southwards slightly marred by massive hangars on the skyline. The church (1837) lies at the south west end of the village, below a pleasant triangular green. It has a lofty interior, which has been most attractively restored, with imaginative painting throughout.

Rodmarton Church

RODMARTON

(6–SE) (4½ miles North East of Tetbury)

This has a small green overlooked by quiet cottages, and an attractively spired church. Pollarded trees create a 'lych-gate' effect over the churchyard gate, and there are several pleasant tombs in the churchyard. Unfortunately the interior was ruthlessly scraped by the Victorians, but there are old stone floors, several handsome 18th and 19th century monuments, and a brass of a lawyer complete with his cap and gown.

SAPPERTON

(6–NE) (5 miles West of Cirencester)

Trim little village poised above the deep Frome valley, with an attractive terrace road beyond the church. This lies at the bottom of a long sloping path beneath yew trees, and is a largely 18th century building, having round headed windows with their original glass, and a very stylish interior including much Jacobean woodwork removed from Sapperton House, which was demolished in about 1730. There are two very fine monuments here....Sir Henry Poole and family (1818), and Sir Robert Atkyns (1711)

Monuments at Sapperton

TARLTON

(6–SE) (4 miles West of Cirencester)

Pleasantly scattered little village with a pretty creeper-covered Post Office. The small 'Norman' church was re-built in 1875, and is not of great interest.

THAMES & SEVERN CANAL (Maps 4–6–9–13)

This was opened in 1789 to link the Stroudwater Canal at Stroud, with the head of the navigable Thames at Lechlade, and was finally abandoned in 1927. Its closure was one of the great tragedies of English Canal history, and although brave efforts are being made to restore certain sections, it is difficult to believe that this outstandingly beautiful link between our two great river systems will ever be re-opened in its entirety.

The Tunnel House Inn

About a mile to the north of Tarlton, there is a 'round house', one of the delightful little 'gothick' towers strung out along the canal, as houses for the length-men (maintenance men). Take a turn northwards from this road, by an inn sign, and go beside the canal 'ditch', here shaded by massive beech trees, to the Tunnel House Inn, a pleasant 18th century building close to the canal tunnel entrance. This 'portal' (restored since we took our photograph) is still embellished by Doric columns and marks the beginning of a 2¼ mile tunnel to Sapperton (see above).

TUNLEY see P 45.

WATERLANE see P 46.

Canal tunnel portal, near the Tunnel House Inn (Restored since this photograph was taken.)

MAP 6

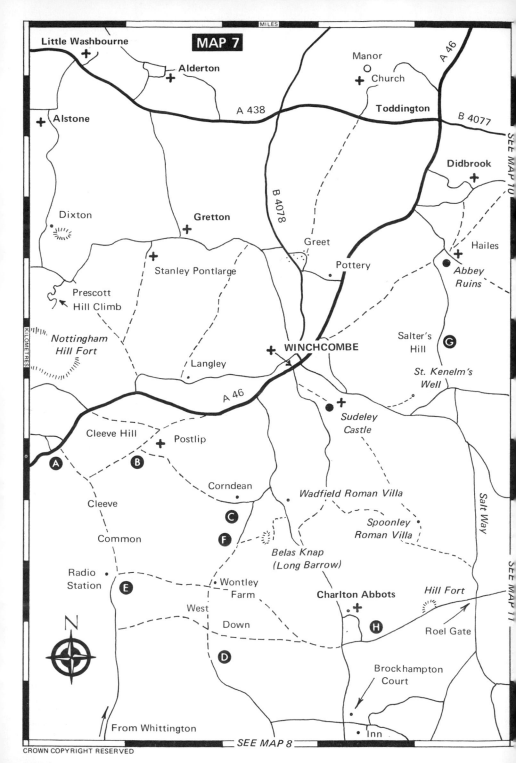

MILES

MAP 7

Little Washbourne

Alderton

Manor
○
✝ Church

A 438

Toddington

A 46

Alstone

B 4077

Didbrook

Dixton

Gretton

B 4078

Greet

Pottery

Hailes

✝
Abbey
Ruins ●

Stanley Pontlarge

Prescott
Hill Climb

Nottingham
Hill Fort

Langley

WINCHCOMBE

Salter's
Hill Ⓖ

St. Kenelm's
Well

A 46

● ✝
Sudeley
Castle

Cleeve Hill

Ⓐ

✝ Postlip

Ⓑ

Corndean

Wadfield Roman Villa

Salt Way

Cleeve

Ⓒ

Spoonley
Roman Villa

Common

Ⓕ

Radio
Station

Ⓔ

Belas Knap
(Long Barrow)

● Wontley
Farm

West

Down

Charlton Abbots

✝

Ⓗ

Hill Fort

Roel Gate

N

Ⓓ

Brockhampton
Court

From Whittington

● Inn

SEE MAP 8

SEE MAP 10

SEE MAP 11

KILOMETRES

Map 7

A Roman Valley and Medieval Abbeys

BELAS KNAP, HAILES ABBEY, SUDELEY CASTLE, WINCHCOMBE, etc. . . .

ALDERTON

(7—NW) (3 miles North West of Winchcombe)
A 'transitional' village, as much 'Avon Valley' as Cotswold' in character, with some half-timbering, some stone, and several thatched roofs. The mainly 14th century church looks pleasant, standing in its tidy churchyard, but the interior was ruthlessly restored in the late 19th century, and is not of great interest to visitors, apart from its long, iron bound chest, which is a fine specimen of medieval craftsmanship.

ALSTONE

(7—NW) (3½ miles North West of Winchcombe)
Here is another transitional village, with a mixture of timber framing and Cotswold stone. It is quietly situated below Woolstone Hill, an outlier of the true Cotswolds. The little church was over-restored by the Victorians, who left the walls coldly scraped and re-pointed; but there is a Norman doorway within the 17th century porch, and the capitals below the chancel arch have interesting Norman detail.

Alstone Church

BELAS KNAP

(7—SW) (2 miles South of Winchcombe)
Stone Age burial mound or 'long barrow', dating from about 2000BC. One of the finest examples in the country, it has been well restored by the Department of the Environment. The restored 'false portal' at the north west end illustrates the great antiquity of the dry stone walling tradition in the Cotswolds. Belas Knap is situated in high country, and can either be reached by walking up ¾ mile from the road between Winchcombe and Charlton Abbots, or by driving up a road leading off Corndean Lane part way towards Wontley Farm, and walking across (see map).

False Portal, Belas Knap

BROCKHAMPTON

(7—SE) (4 miles South of Winchcombe)
Hamlet with a large, mainly 19th century mansion, Brockhampton Park, and an inn called the Craven Arms, very tucked away. The lovely River Colne, a tributary of the Thames, rises just to the north of Brockhampton, and in Charlton Abbots, a mile beyond, the Isbourne starts its journey towards the Avon at Evesham.....high watershed country this.

CHARLTON ABBOTS

(7—SE) (2½ miles South of Winchcombe)
Hamlet with a magnificent manor house and a small church, from whose churchyard there are fine views out over the 'Sudeley valley'. The church was re-built in the 19th century, and is not of great interest.

Charlton Abbots Manor

Above Corndean — Map Ref. **F**

CLEEVE HILL and CLEEVE COMMON

(7—SW) (2½ miles West of Winchcombe)
This great expanse of open common land is the Cotswold's highest point (1082 feet), and is grand country over which to walk or ride. There are splendid views out over the Severn plain to the Malverns, May Hill, and the Welsh mountains beyond. The best access points are from Cleeve Hill village [A] (on the A 46), Postlip [B], Corndean Lane [C], West Down [D], and the radio station three miles north of Whittington [E]

CORNDEAN HALL

(7—SW) (1½ miles South of Winchcombe)
Pleasant 18th century house visible from Corndean Lane, one of the points of access to Cleeve Common (see above).

DIDBROOK

(7—NE) (3 miles North East of Winchcombe)
Small village below the hills with a pleasant mixture of timber and stone in its buildings.....see especially the several examples of 'cruck' contruction in various cottage ends.....possibly as early as the 15th century. The church was re-built about 1475 by an abbot of Hailes and is wholly Perpendicular in style. See especially the lovely old roof, the various old wood furnishings, and the very unusual 'descent' of the tower into the nave, with three open arches.

Road to Didbrook

DIXTON

(7—NW) (2½ miles North West of Winchcombe)
Hamlet to the south of Alstone, with a fine 16th century manor house, and above it, the earthworks of a probable Iron Age hill fort on Dixton Hill.

GREET

(7—NE) (1 mile North of Winchcombe)
A large hamlet to the immediate north of Winchcombe with a pleasant manor farmhouse, complete with a 17th century dovecot, and a half-timbered house opposite. However these items of interest have been rather over shadowed by a quantity of modern development.

A short distance to the east, near the A 46, is the WINCHCOMBE POTTERY, which has been creating excellent craft work for many years (having been revived by Michael Cardew in the thirties). There is a modest shop, and we suspect that real enthusiasts would be allowed to watch the potters at work.

Didbrook Church

GRETTON

(7—NW) (1½ miles North West of Winchcombe)
A small 'black and white' (half-timbered) village situated beneath nine hundred foot high Langley Hill. The church is not, in our view, one of the more inspiring Victorian buildings we have encountered, although great care and attention was obviously lavished upon its design. We must confess that we failed to spot the tower of the otherwise demolished medieval church which apparently stands amongst black and white cottages nearer the centre of the village, but we are assured that it is 'very prettily situated'.

At Winchcombe Pottery, near Greet

MAP 7   34

HAILES ABBEY and HAILES

(7–NE) (2 miles North East of Winchcombe)
Here beneath the Cotswold edge, are the remains of an abbey founded in 1246, by Richard, Earl of Cornwall, who had vowed to do so, following his escape from a shipwreck off the Scilly Isles. This was colonised by monks from Beaulieu in Hampshire, a Cistercian house founded by Richard's father, King John. Hailes' popularity as a place of pilgrimage was then assured by Richard's son Edmund who gave the monks a relic of the 'Holy Blood' authenticated by the Pope himself.

Christmas Eve 1539 witnessed the final surrender of the Abbey to the agents of Henry VIII, and all that now remains, are parts of the cloisters and various low walls. However, the plan of the magnificent abbey church has been perpetuated by the planting of trees, and the site is well worth visiting. There is an interesting museum containing many medieval tiles, a beautiful series of roof bosses, life size figures of Cistercian monks, and many other finds from the excavations of the abbey.

The little parish church of Hailes is nearly a hundred years older than the abbey, although its windows are mainly 14th century. There are old stone floors, medieval wall paintings and stained glass, a 15th century rood screen, and attractive 17th century woodwork. The church was restored in 1961 with great sympathy, and is still full of an atmosphere of the past.

From Hailes there is an interesting road southwards, up over the Cotswold edge, following an ancient 'salt way' (hill known as Salter's Hill). There is also an attractive bridle-way up to Farmcote (P 53) and footpaths to Winchcombe, Didbrook and Wood Stanway.

Road near Salter's Hill (see Hailes) — Map Ref. Ⓖ

Hailes Abbey

LITTLE WASHBOURNE

(7–NW) (4 miles North West of Winchcombe)
Small hamlet with minute Norman church prettily sited in an orchard, with white bell cote and a completely unspoilt Georgian interior. There is a Norman chancel arch and a Norman lancet window in the chancel, but the attractions of Little Washbourne church are its two-decker pulpit, its lovely 18th century box pews each with its own candle holder (no nonsense with electricity here). If you relish a quiet journey back to the simplicity of 18th century England, sit quietly for a while in this delightful little building.

Little Washbourne Church

POSTLIP

(7–SW) (1 mile West of Winchcombe)
Fine Jacobean manor house charmingly situated at the head of a valley below Cleeve Common, with a small Norman chapel (now Roman Catholic) in its grounds. There is a Norman south doorway and chancel arch, and a 16th century nave roof.

PRESCOTT

(7–NW) (2½ miles West of Winchcombe)
Small hamlet beneath steep Nottingham Hill, which is itself topped with the ramparts of an Iron Age hill fort. Prescott is renowned throughout the world of motor sport as the site of Prescott Hill Climb. This is operated by the Bugatti Owners' Club and meetings are held here about five times each year.

Two-Decker Pulpit, Little Washbourne

MAP 7

Sheep Country near Roel Gate — Map Ref. 🅗

Stanley Pontlarge Church

Norman Chancel Arch, Stanley Pontlarge

Sudeley Castle

ROEL GATE and THE SALT WAY

(7—SE) (3 miles South East of Winchcombe)
Lonely cross roads about nine hundred feet above sea level, with fine views north towards Winchcombe. There is a seat here in memory of 'Arthur Edwin Boycott.....Pathologist, Naturalist and Friend 1877—1938'.....at what better place could one wish to be remembered?

Roel Gate is on the 'Salt Way' running southwards past Hailes Abbey to Hazleton. Should you wish to study this in more detail we would recommend the Ordnance Survey 1:50,000 maps of the Cotswold area. We believe this particular Salt Way linked the salt producing town of Droitwich with the head of the navigable Thames at Lechlade, from where the salt could easily be moved down river to London.

There is an Iron Age hill fort at Grim's Hill, half a mile to the west of Roel Gate, astride the road to Charlton Abbots, but its earthworks are not of great interest.

ST. KENELM'S WELL

(7—SE) (1 mile East of Winchcombe)
This is a 19th century reconstruction of a Holy Well connected with St. Kenelm, the martyred boy prince (A.D. 819), whose shrine brought such great prosperity to Winchcombe Abbey. The well lies about ¼ mile north of the road up from Winchcombe beyond Sudeley Castle. The footpath is muddy and it is not signed.....but the views are worthwhile.

SPOONLEY ROMAN VILLA

(7—SE) (2 miles South East of Winchcombe)
Situated in a wood about ¾ mile north west of Roel Gate, are the remains of a Roman villa excavated in the late 19th century. This lies on private property, although there appears to be a public footpath through the woods close by. It is a great pity that the remains of this delightfully situated villa have not been properly protected, especially as its 'courtyard' layout plan was used to illustrate that classic text-book, 'Everyday Life in Roman Britain'.

STANLEY PONTLARGE

(7—NW) (2 miles North West of Winchcombe)
Hamlet beneath Langley Hill, with a small Norman church. This has a Norman north doorway and chancel arch, but most of the remaining 'Norman' features are Victorian copies. Despite its quiet setting this church lacks the atmosphere we had hoped for.

SUDELEY CASTLE

(7—SE) (½ mile South East of Winchcombe)
Beautifully sited building dating partly from the 15th century, looking across a valley towards the wooded slopes of Cleeve Hill. Its history is too complex to relate here, but Catherine Parr, the sixth wife of Henry VIII came here on the king's death in 1547, as the wife of her former lover, Lord Seymour, but died in childbirth the following year. She is buried in the 15th century church.

The castle and church were badly damaged in the Civil War, and it was only in the 19th century that both came to be used again. The interior of the church is therefore rather Victorian in feeling, but the lovely Perpendicular exterior has survived intact. The castle was also extensively restored and partly re-built in the

MAP 7　　　　36

19th century, but it is nevertheless full of interest to visitors. Do not miss the beautifully displayed collection of toys, the largest private collection in the country.

TODDINGTON

(7—NE) (3½ miles North East of Winchcombe)
Toddington 'New Town' is an unexceptional modern development, with inn, shop and garage at a roundabout on the A 46. But tucked quietly away in a wooded area to the north-west is an impressive 19th century church built by our favourite Victorian architect, G.E. Street. It is a combination of starkness and extravagance, which is summarised in the white marble tomb of Charles Hanbury-Tracy and his wife. Toddington Manor, which can be glimpsed from the churchyard, was built to the design of the same Charles Hanbury-Tracy....a splendid Victorian Gothic mansion, which is not however open to the public.

Hanbury-Tracy Monument, Toddington

WADFIELD ROMAN VILLA

(7—SE) (1½ miles South of Winchcombe)
Another Roman villa excavated in the 19th century, with a small hut covering a mosaic pavement, on private property, in a small wood to the immediate east of the Winchcombe—Charlton Abbots road.

WINCHCOMBE

(7—NE) (6 miles North East of Cheltenham)
Attractive small town sheltered on three sides by the high wolds. Winchcombe's prosperity in medieval times was due to its abbey.....founded in 798 by King Kenulf of Mercia, and soon after dedicated to Kenulf's martyred son St. Kenelm. Although this event is now believed to be the fabrication of a later period, it brought pilgrims in great quantity to the shrine of St. Kenelm, and stood the monks and citizens of Winchcombe in good stead for several hundred years.

Winchcombe

The fine Perpendicular wool church was built jointly by town (the nave) and abbey (the chancel), but despite its connection with the abbey, it survived the 'dissolution' entirely. The great abbey was otherwise completely destroyed by Lord Seymour of Sudeley, and the only reminder of its past glories is the George Inn, which was once a hostel for pilgrims.

Winchcombe's streets are full of character, despite the busy A 46, and we particularly like the picturesque group of almshouses by Sir Gilbert Scott.

House at Uley (See Map 1)

MAP 1 continued from P 9.

ULEY

(1—SE) (2 miles East of Dursley)
Large village with many delightful 18th century houses.....evidence of Uley's prosperity as a cloth centre immediately prior to the Industrial Revolution. The Victorian church is well sited above the road, and there is a path up from it, to Uleybury, an extensive Iron Age hill fort, from whence there are fine views.

ULEY TUMULUS (or Hetty Pegler's Tump)

(1—SE) (1 mile North of Uley)
A Stone Age, chambered long barrow, the eastern end of which can be explored. The very low entrance is kept locked, but the key may be collected from the cottage on the hill up from Uley. (Take torch and old clothes.)

Entrance to Uley Tumulus (See Map 1)

MAP 7

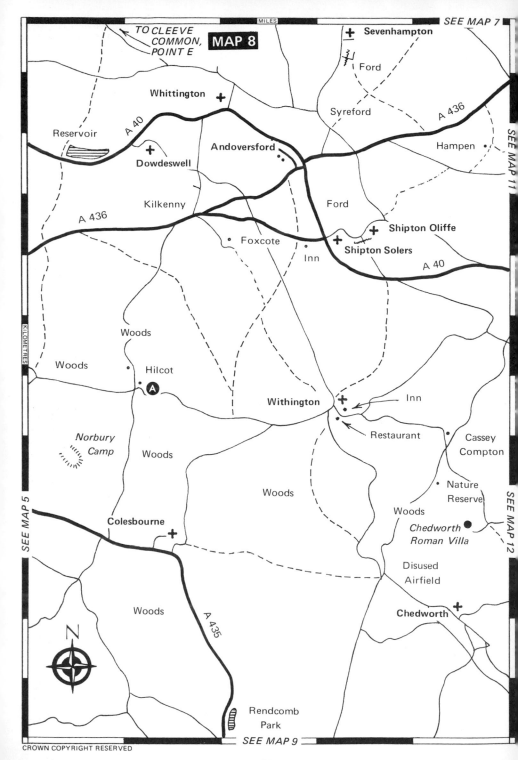

MILES

TO CLEEVE
COMMON,
POINT E

MAP 8

Sevenhampton

Ford

Whittington

A 40

Syreford

A 436

Reservoir

Hampen

Dowdeswell

Andoversford

Kilkenny

A 436

Ford

Foxcote

Shipton Oliffe

Inn

Shipton Solers

A 40

Woods

Woods

Hilcot

Ⓐ

Withington

Inn

Norbury
Camp

Restaurant

Cassey
Compton

Woods

Nature
Reserve

Woods

Woods

Chedworth
Roman Villa

Colesbourne

Disused
Airfield

Chedworth

N

Woods

A 435

KILOMETRES

Rendcomb
Park

Map 8

Secret Woodlands and a Roman Villa

CHEDWORTH, COLESBORNE, WHITTINGTON, WITHINGTON, etc. . . .

ANDOVERSFORD
(8—NE) (5 miles East of Cheltenham)
An indeterminate village, now happily by-passed by the busy A 40, which makes use of an old railway line. No special features.

CASSEY COMPTON
(8—SE) (4 miles West of Northleach)
Partly demolished 17th century mansion, now a large farmhouse, lying in the wooded valley of the Coln below Withington, with open roads and wooded verges offering pleasant picnic possibilities. The house and its surroundings now bear few signs of their former elegance, and it is perhaps for this very reason that we are so attracted by it.

Cassey Compton Manor

CHEDWORTH VILLAGE
(8—SE) (4 miles South West of Northleach)
Large village, once neatly dissected by a branch line, complete with tall viaduct, and whose closure only the most fanatical railway enthusiast could deplore. The attractive part of the village centres upon the Seven Tuns Inn, the spring bubbling out of a wall opposite, and the interesting late Norman church a short distance beyond. This was considerably enriched during the Perpendicular period, and light floods in through tall windows on the south side, on to the stout Norman tub font, and (in contrast) on to the elegant 15th century stone pulpit. Do not miss the lovely modern sculpture of a Virgin and Child (1911).

CHEDWORTH ROMAN VILLA
(8—SE) (3½ miles West of Northleach)
Situated in a beautifully wooded stretch of the Coln valley, this is without doubt, Britain's most attractive Roman villa. It owes its discovery in 1864 to an over ambitious ferret which had to be dug out of a rabbit warren, thus revealing various mosaic fragments. The villa is now owned by the National Trust, who maintain the interesting remains and an excellent small museum. The delightful woodland setting proves once again how adept the Romans were in the siting of their villas.

At Chedworth Roman Villa

COLESBORNE
(8—SW) (6 miles South East of Cheltenham)
The church has a fine Perpendicular tower and is one of only about sixty churches in the whole country to possess a medieval stone pulpit (many of which are in the Cotswolds). The number of exotic trees to be

Pulpit at Chedworth

Colesbourne Church

MAP 8

Dowdeswell Church

found in the park surrounding the church, is due to th
planting activities of Squire Henry Elwes (1846–1922)
soldier, big-game hunter, botanist and, above al
forester. Elwes roamed the world in search of exoti
tree specimens, and brought these back to be establish
ed in his park at Colesborne.

DOWDESWELL

(8–NW) (3 miles East of Cheltenham
Agreeably sited on a hillside, and happily just awa
from the busy A 40. The church, with its small ston
spire is situated below the road, beside a Tudor farm
house. Inside there are two mid-19th century galleries
one for the manor and one for the rectory; a 16th
century brass of a priest and a handsome monument o
the chancel wall (William Rogers, 1734).

FOXCOTE

(8–NW) (4 miles South East of Cheltenham
Small hamlet about a mile to the south west of And
oversford, with a 17th century manor house just to it
south. There is a pleasant path southwards from
Foxcote to Withington.

HAMPEN

(8–NE) (6½ miles East of Cheltenham
Very quiet hamlet which is best approached south
wards from the A 436. There is a pleasant bridle-road
from Salperton, and one can walk on south and wes
to Shipton Oliffe, by using a combination of path
road, and further bridle-road.

Farm at Hilcot — Map Ref. Ⓐ

HILCOT WOOD and PINCHLEY WOOD

(8–SW) (5 miles South East of Cheltenham
A delightful, little known area of woodland in a valle
which gives birth to the Hilcot brook, a tributary o
the Churn. Upper Hilcot farmhouse is half timbered..
an unusual feature in this countryside of Cotswolc
stone.

NORBURY CAMP

(8–SW) (5 miles South East of Cheltenham
Iron Age hill fort about a mile to the north-north-wes
of Colesborne. (No public access.)

SEVENHAMPTON

(8–NE) (4 miles South of Winchcombe
Has a small ford in a valley overlooked by modest cott
ages, and nearer our road, a Norman church, altered
and improved by the benefaction of John Camber, a
rich wool merchant, who died in 1497. Flowering rock
plants line the path to the south door, and inside
John Camber's Perpendicular tower has provided
another fascinating architectural story, with flying
buttresses within the church, and vaulting high up
above the crossing.

Cottage at Sevenhampton

SHIPTON OLIFFE

(8–NE) (6 miles East of Cheltenham
Long village on a small tributary of the Coln, with a
minute ford, a startling Methodist chapel in bright red
brick, and a pretty church overlooking ornamenta
gardens by the stream. It has all been rather tidied up
inside, but we particularly liked the colourful Roya
Arms in plaster relief.

Ford at Shipton Oliffe

MAP 8   40

SHIPTON SOLERS

(8—NE) (5½ miles East of Cheltenham)
Smaller than Oliffe, but the manor house's stream-side
gardens are equally enchanting, and the little church,
which is situated just above the road, was very sympathetically restored in 1929. This is usually locked, but
is well worth visiting. The comfortable Frog Mill Inn,
was a well used coaching halt on the Gloucester—
London road, and has now once again come into its
own (hotel and restaurant).

At Shipton Sollers

SYREFORD

(8—NE) (5 miles South of Winchcombe)
Has a pleasant mill house, but otherwise there are no
special features in this small hamlet north of Andoversford. A Roman settlement was excavated here many
years ago, and amongst the items recovered was a
delightful four inch high statuette of Mars.

WHITTINGTON

(8—NW) (4 miles East of Cheltenham)
Here are pleasant rows of cottages, a Victorian wayside
well inscribed 'Waste not, want not', and, well away
from the village a small church sheltering beneath the
high walls of the romantic 16th century Whittington
Court. The church, which has some Norman details,
has a small bellcote and a pretty little north porch.
However the most interesting treasures here are the
three 14th century effigies, with two knights and one
lady. Do not miss the brass to Richard Cotton and his
wife, the builders of Whittington Court; nor the two
little head stops to the arcading.....a lady and gentleman, who both look most Chaucerian. It all seems very
remote from the hot dogs and hamburgers available on
the A 40 lay-by a few yards away.

There is a good access point to Cleeve Common
(P 34) at the end of a road west and north from
Whittington, by a radio station. (Distance from
Whittington 3.6 miles.)

Whittington Court

WITHINGTON

(8—SE) (5 miles West of Northleach)
A pleasant, bustling village situated near the head of
the beautiful Coln valley. There is a large church with
partly Norman tower, blocked Norman north doorway,
and fine Norman south doorway. The interior has been
over restored, but don't miss the wall monument to
Sir John and Lady Howe of Cassey Compton, complete with their eight children. We have fond memories
of vast log fires, shove-halfpenny, and excellent bread
and cheese, at the hospitable Mill Inn. Nearby Halewell Close
is an exceptionally comfortable country-house hotel.

The Mill Inn, Withington

MAP 3 continued from P 17.

WHADDON

(3—NW) (3 miles North West of Painswick)
Scrappy little village to the north west of the M 5. The
church looks most attractive from the outside, but the
Victorians ruined the flavour of the interior. However
do not overlook the 20th century east window (by
Sir Ninian Comper), nor the colourful Royal Arms of
George III.

WHITESHILL

(3—SW) (1 mile North of Stroud)
Long village straggling up the hill out of Stroud, with
fine views but an unexceptional Victorian church.

Howe Monument, Withington

MAP 8

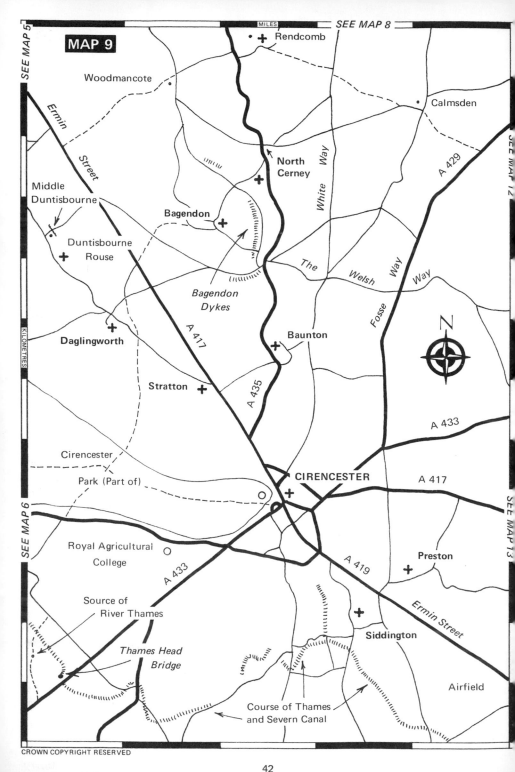

MAP 9

SEE MAP 5
SEE MAP 8
SEE MAP 12
SEE MAP 13
SEE MAP 6

MILES

Rendcomb
Woodmancote
Calmsden
Ermin Street
North Cerney
White Way
Middle Duntisbourne
Bagendon
Duntisbourne Rouse
A 429
Bagendon Dykes
The Welsh Way
Fosse Way
Daglingworth
A 417
Baunton
N
Stratton
A 435
A 433
Cirencester
Park (Part of)
CIRENCESTER
A 417
Royal Agricultural College
A 433
A 419
Preston
Source of River Thames
Siddington
Thames Head Bridge
Ermin Street
Airfield
Course of Thames and Severn Canal

KILOMETRES

Map 9

Roman Roads and the Birthplace of the Thames

CIRENCESTER, DUNTISBOURNE ROUSE, NORTH CERNEY, THAMES HEAD, etc. . . .

BAGENDON

(9—NW) (3 miles North of Cirencester)
Small village in a sheltered valley. The over-restored church is all on a very small scale, with Norman saddle-back tower and Norman arcading. The chancel is much higher than the nave, and was made so in medieval times to avoid flooding. See especially the handsome little 'Rector's Roll', and the window in the north wall of the chancel. Bagendon Dykes, to the south and west of the village, are the remains of the Belgic (Iron Age) capital of the Dobunni, which flourished here immediately before the coming of the Romans, who 'civilized' the tribes by moving them into Roman style provincial capitals.....in this case Cirencester (Corinium Dobunn-orum).

Bagendon Church

BAUNTON

(9—NE) (2 miles North of Cirencester)
Straggling village to the immediate north of Cirencester, and too close to preserve much of its individuality. However the small church lies quietly away from the main road. It has a heavily restored interior, but should not be missed, as it contains a remarkable 14th century wall painting of St. Christopher. See also the richly embroidered 15th century altar frontal.

CALMSDEN

(9—NE) (5 miles North East of Cirencester)
Agreeable little hamlet with a row of attractively glazed early 19th century cottages, and a 14th century wayside cross.

Cirencester

CIRENCESTER

(9—SE) (12 miles East of Stroud)
Busy market town, standing on the site of Corinium, Roman Britain's second largest city. Meeting point of the Fosse Way, Ermin Street and Akeman Street over 1800 years ago, Cirencester still thrives today as the centre of life in the southern Cotswolds.

Many of the gaily coloured shops in the Market Square retain their individuality and charm, and over all presides the magnificent Perpendicular tower and porch of the Parish Church. This fine 15th century 'wool church' has a splendid roof illuminated by clerestory windows, medieval stained glass in the east and west windows, a painted 'wine glass' pulpit, and also many fine brasses. See also the surviving arcade of St. John's Hospital (founded by Henry II) in Spitalgate Street, and the really excellent Corinium Museum in Park Street.

St. John's Hospital, Cirencester

MAP 9

Cirencester Park, Town Entrance

CIRENCESTER PARK

(9—SW & 6—NE) (Immediately to West of Cirenceste
The mansion (which lies at the town end of the par
was built by the First Earl Bathurst in 1714—18, and
not open to the public. However, as for the par
notices proclaim *'You are welcome on foot and c
horseback by permission of the Earl Bathurst. Dog
cars, cycles or unaccompanied children are not allowe
Take your litter home'*. The Broad Ride is nearly fi
miles long and stretches westwards from the tow
almost to Sapperton (P 31). Wander at will in gre
woodlands and open parkland, but always rememb
that you are a privileged guest, and not there by righ
Use O.S. 1:50,000 Map No. 163 to explore properly.

DAGLINGWORTH

(9—NW) (3 miles North West of Cirenceste
The charmingly sited church and rectory stand we
above the rest of the village. The church has a Saxo
doorway, and part of a Roman altar, re-used by th
Saxons, who made it into a window. The three carvin
set into the walls were rediscovered in 1850 and form
unique group of primitive Saxon sculpture. See als
the interesting Saxon sundial over the doorway, an
the fine 15th century door itself.

Daglingworth Church

DUNTISBOURNE ROUSE

(9—NW) (4 miles North West of Cirenceste
A mainly Norman church standing in a sloping churc
yard, with a fine 14th century cross for company.
has a pleasing interior, with box pews, stalls in th
chancel with misericords, and medieval wall painting
It is interesting to find that this is built upon such
slope, that there is a crypt at its eastern end.....a mo
unusual feature in so small a church.

FOSSE WAY

(Maps 6—9—12—15—1
This is Britain's best known Roman road, and extende
from Exeter to Lincoln. Its line marked the conclusio
of the first stage of the Roman invasion of Britain an
consolidation of Roman gains in south and east wer
made before any substantial occupation was carried ou
in the areas to its north and west.

MIDDLE DUNTISBOURNE

(9—NW) (4 miles North West of Cirenceste
Disappointing hamlet with a rather deep ford overlook
ed by scrappy farm buildings, some with untidy corru
gated iron roofs.

Sculpture at Daglingworth

North Cerney Church

NORTH CERNEY

(9—NE) (4 miles North of Cirenceste
Pleasant village in the Churn valley, with the Bathur
Arms set in a streamside garden, and looking across th
busy A 435 to the little saddle-back tower of th
largely Norman church. This is an exquisitely restore
and re-furnished building, thanks to the generosity c
Mr. W.I. Croome. Much of this work was carried ou
by F.C. Eden, whose work we first encountered a
Blisland on the remote western fringes of Bodmi
Moor. See especially the Norman south doorway, th
roof with its fascinating corbel figures, the handsom
gallery, the fine stone pulpit, the beautiful medieva
glass, and the lovely monument to Thomas Tyndale i
the Lady Chapel. See also the late 17th centur
Rectory opposite, and Cerney House beyond.

Duntisbourne Rouse Church

MAP 9   44

PRESTON

(9—SE) (1 mile South East of Cirencester)
The small church is approached by a narrow pathway
bordered with pollarded limes. The 14th century triple
bellcote is worth noting, although we spent more time
gazing in envy at the gorgeous farmhouse next door.

RENDCOMB

(9—NW) (5 miles North of Cirencester)
Has an Italianate mansion and an interesting church,
both overlooking the Churn valley. The church is a largely Perpendicular building thanks to the munificence
of Sir Edmund Tame, wool merchant of Fairford, and
son of John Tame, who built the magnificent church
here. See especially the stained glass, the 16th century
screen (an unusual feature in the Cotswolds), and above
all, the splendid Norman font with figures of the
apostles beneath arcades, with Judas left uncarved.

Farm near the Church, Preston

SIDDINGTON

(9—SE) (1 mile South East of Cirencester)
Now almost a suburb of Cirencester, Siddington has
managed to preserve its individuality in the area immediately surrounding the tall spired church. Much of this
was re-built by the Victorians, but there is a splendid
Norman south doorway with a tympanum depicting
Christ in Majesty, a beautiful Perpendicular north aisle
chapel with a fine roof supported on angle corbels,
and an unusually tall font which may have been used for
adult baptisms? Do not miss the pleasant 16th century
barn overlooking the churchyard.

Christ in Majesty, Siddington

THAMES HEAD

(9—SW) (3 miles South West of Cirencester)
It is a fine walk across the fields to Trewsbury Mead,
either from Coates, or from the Thames Head Inn.
However be prepared for an anti-climax, as you will
probably find nothing more than a muddy depression
beneath a tree, with a granite slab proclaiming this to
be the source of the Thames. This stone replaces a
handsome statue of Neptune which has been removed
to St. John's Lock below Lechlade (See Buscot, Page
9), as it sadly became the subject of vandalism within
a short time of its arrival here in 1958.
Do not overlook the 'earthworks' of the Thames &
Severn Canal, which used to run close by.

THE WHITE WAY

(9—NE, etc.) (North from Cirencester)
A minor Roman road serving the various villas that lay
between Cirencester and the Cotswold edge in the
vicinity of Winchcombe.

Rendcomb Font

MAP 6 continued from P 31.

BUNLEY

(6—NW) (5 miles East of Stroud)
Small hamlet in a deeply wooded combe thrusting
northwards from the Frome valley.

WATERLANE

(6—NW) (4½ miles East of Stroud)
A scattered hamlet with some rather indifferent
dwellings, in high country to the north of Oakridge.

Rendcomb Church

Rendcomb Font (detail)

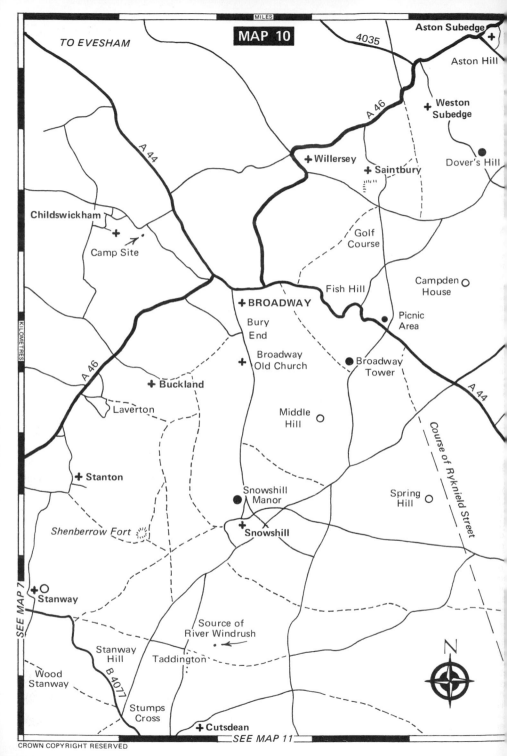

Map 10

Some North Cotswold Classics

BROADWAY, DOVER'S HILL, SNOWSHILL, STANTON, STANWAY, etc. . . .

ASTON SUBEDGE

(10—NE) (4 miles North East of Broadway)
Small, unspoilt village beneath the Cotswold edge, with
houses, farms and little church amongst orchards
which were white with blossom when we last called
here). The church was built in 1797 and, rather unusually, shows signs of Greek influence in its bell turret
and cornice. Inside there is a minute gallery with a
charming old clock, and a canopied pulpit, both
contemporary with the church itself.

Opposite the church there is a lovely,17th century
manor house, once the home of Endymion Porter
1587—1649). Porter, an ambassador of Charles I,
entertained Prince Rupert here when he came to the
Cotswold Games organized by Porter's friend, Captain
Robert Dover (see Dover's Hill, P 49).

A short distance away there are several other attractive houses and cottages, with a small stream beside the
road, below pleasantly wooded Aston Hill.

At Aston Subedge

BROADWAY

(10 NW) (5 miles South East of Evesham)
One of England's show villages, Broadway has a fine
wide street bordered with trim greens and a bewilder-
ingly beautiful series of old stone houses, largely dating
from the 17th and 18th centuries All of this sits
comfortably below the Cotswold edge and is overlooked by the stone built folly of Broadway Tower (P 48).

Broadway's praises have been sung for very many
years, and accordingly a fair proportion of its fine
houses are now devoted to the needs of its visitors.....
with hotels and antique shops much in evidence.
However it still retains a very real degree of charm and
interest, and despite traffic from the A 44 and A 46,
its character remains intact.

If possible drive or walk, out on the Snowshill road,
past the handsomely towered Victorian 'new' church,
past the old houses of Bury End, to the 'old' church
of St. Eadburgha's. This lies in a quite valley leading
into the hills about a mile to the south of the village,
looking out over a small stream at the bottom of the
churchyard. It is a cruciform building with Norman
origins and has a delightfully unspoilt interior, which
is full of atmosphere. The Victorians no doubt con-
centrated all their energies on the building of the new
church and left St. Eadburgha's undisturbed.

*Picton House,
Broadway*

*Lygon Arms,
Broadway*

Austin House, Broadway

Broadway Tower

Summer at Buckland

Cross at Childswickham

Taddington, near Cutsdean

BROADWAY TOWER

(10—NE) (1 mile South East of Broadway (1023 feet above sea level.) Built in the year 1800 by the Earl of Coventry, who lived at Croome Court about 15 miles to the north west, this gothick folly is an outstanding landmark to those who live in the Severn and Avon valleys. It is one of England's finest viewpoints, and on a clear day, fourteen counties are visible from its castellated roof, with the massive out line of the Black Mountains in the far west, and the long line of the Berkshire Downs to the south.

Bibliophile, Sir Thomas Philipps had a private printing press here between 1822 and 1862, and some years later, William Morris is believed to have spen several weeks lodging here with his friends Burne-Jones and Rossetti. Our own memories are of Mr. and Mrs Hollington, for long the custodians of this windy and often lonely tower.....two warm hearted and friendly souls, who always made us welcome when we called this way.

Broadway Tower is now the central feature of a 'Country Park', and its facilities include car park reception building (shop and restaurant) picnic area exhibitions in the nearby tower barn and in the tower itself and finally a woodland nature walk.

BUCKLAND

(10—NW) (1½ miles South West of Broadway Delightfully situated little village at the end of a road leading up into a combe in the hills. There is a pleasant bridle-way up over the hills to Snowshill. It has an interesting church containing 15th century glass, some splendid 17th century canopied seating, and a pulpit of the same period. The lovely rectory dates from the 15th century and is the oldest medieval parsonage still in use in the county (see Times of Admission) The manor house was much restored in the 19th cent ury, but it now has a shop and also offers pony trekking.

CHILDSWICKHAM

(10—NW) (1½ miles North West of Broadway This is a patchy village lying well away from the Cots wold edge, with the inevitable mixture of stone, half timber and brick. However there are quiet paths and roadways leading to the church, and a little triangula green complete with old cross, beyond a stream. The church has a fine tall spire and a Norman west door way, but the interior has been over restored. There i an extensive caravan and camping site to the south eas of the village.

CUTSDEAN

(10—SW) (4½ miles South of Broadway Small upland village on the slopes of the Windrush valley, less than a mile below its source at Field Barn Taddington. Its church lies beyond a large farmyard and is a long narrow Victorian building, with a medie val tower providing the only item of interest. When we last called here, half the churchyard was wired off, to allow sheep to graze amongst the grave-stones.....a truly Cotswold solution to the ever present problem of churchyard maintenance.

MAP 10   48

DOVER'S HILL

(10—NE) (1 mile North West of Chipping Campden)
This fine open field walk along the crescent shaped hillside (owned by the National Trust) was the site of the famous Cotswold Games, founded by Robert Dover during the reign of James I. Although temporarily suppressed during the Cromwellian period they were otherwise held regularly each year until 1851. They were then discontinued owing to the riotous behaviour of Irish navvies, who were then building the nearby Campden railway tunnel, and who must have adored the noble sport of shin-kicking.....one of the favourite Cotswold 'games'.

The games have recently been revived yet again, but for us, Dover's Hill is best remembered for its splendid views out over the Avon valley and the distant Midland Plain (aided by a viewing topograph).

On Dover's Hill

FISH HILL

(10—NE) (½ mile East of Broadway)
A long winding hill out of Broadway, and up to the top of the Cotswold edge by the Fish Inn, an amusing little stone building. There is an extensive Picnic Area to the north of the cross roads just beyond the top of the hill.

LAVERTON

(10—SW) (2 miles South West of Broadway)
Large hamlet beneath the Cotswold scarp, with an attractive Post Office stores and several pleasant farmhouses. There are paths to Buckland and Stanton, and a pleasant bridle-way up the hill.

RYKNIELD STREET

(Maps 10 and 15)
An important Roman road running northwards from the Fosse Way near Bourton-on-the-Water, past Condicote, down the Cotswold edge between Saintbury and Weston Subedge, to Bidford, Alcester, Birmingham and Derby, and ending at Templeborough near Sheffield. The best section for walking is southwards from Condicote (P 70), although It is also possible to walk up the hill from the A 46 beyond Weston Subedge.

SAINTBURY

(10—NE) (2 miles North East of Broadway)
Small village poised on the slopes of the Cotswolds, with a single street leading down from the church to the main road, where there is a medieval wayside cross. We obtained fine views from the porch of this beautifully spired church, and passing through the Norman north doorway, we were delighted with the equally pleasing interior. See especially the 15th century font, with its attractively shaped 18th century cover, the lovely old nave roof and the 18th century box pews.

Saintbury Church

SNOWSHILL

(10—SW) (2½ miles South of Broadway)
A village with hardly a pair of roof lines on the same level, Snowshill looks out over the Avon valley, and the Midland Plain beyond, from a quiet hillside setting. Its church is of little interest, but The Manor House provides a most unusual experience. Owned by the National Trust, it is a charming Tudor building with a 'William and Mary' front. Its attractive terraced gardens overlook farmlands which rise beyond the combe. The house is packed from ground floor to attic with a fascinating collection of byegones.....toys, musical instruments, weaver's and spinner's tools, clocks, and even bicycles. Do not miss this.

Snowshill Manor

MAP 10

Stanton

Stanton Church

War Memorial Stanway

STANTON

(10—SW) (3 miles South West of Broadwa
An outstandingly beautiful village below the wooded
Cotswold edge, lovingly restored by Sir Philip Stott
the first quarter of the present century. His ow
house, Stanton Court, is a fine Jacobean house, an
rather outshines the 16th century manor house; bu
almost every house in Stanton is a delight to the ey

The church has a well proportioned Perpendicula
tower and spire, and a very attractive two storeye
porch with pinnacles and battlements. Inside, its No
man origins are revealed by the north arcade, and the
are the remains of wall paintings in the north transep
There are two pulpits.....a Jacobean one, and a la
14th century one, no longer used. The church wa
lovingly re-furnished by one of our favourite 20t
century restorers, Sir Ninian Comper, and his wor
has enhanced the atmosphere of an already beautif
medieval interior.

Walk beyond the old wayside cross, up the qui
village street, and on up to the hospitable little Moun
Inn, which awaits you on its small knoll below th
wooded hillside.

From the south of the village, there is a bridle-wa
up the hill to Shenberrow, an extensive Iron Age h
fort, from where one can walk eastwards to Snowshi
or south almost as far as Stumps Cross, turning righ
and down through woods to Stanway.

STANWAY

(10—SW) (4 miles South West of Broadwa
This small village lies at the foot of the beautifully wooded
Stanway Hill, with thatched stone cottages and the attractiv
Old Bakehouse Restaurant between the hill and the cros
roads, where stands the lovely war memorial depicting S
George slaying the Dragon. A short distance to the nort
of this cross roads stands the church, the manor hous
(Stanway House), and its splendid 17th century gatehouse
The church was over restored in the late 19th century, bu
there is a Jacobean pulpit and a beautiful little bronze b
Alexander Fisher (the sculptor of St. George and the Dragon
Stanway House is a handsome Jacobean manor hous
containing fine period furniture, including a workin
shuffleboard table and Chinese Chippendale day-beds. Th
house stands in lovely gardens beneath steep woode
parklands enhanced by an 18th century stone pyramid, fron
whose base a cascade once descended. The gatehouse i
an entrancing piece of architecture, so beautiful that it wa
once thought to have been the work of Inigo Jones. It i
however now thought to have been the work of Timoth
Strong of Great Barrington, one of the outstanding Cotswol
masons and quarry-owners, and kinsman of Thomas Stron
who built the bridge over the Windrush at Great Barringtor
Timothy also worked as a contractor under the direction c
the great Nicholas Stone at Cornbury Park, and it seems like
that some of Stone's influence was felt at Stanway.

Gatehouse, Stanway

WESTON SUBEDGE

(10—NE) (3 miles North East of Broadwa
There are several attractive stone houses in this villag
and at least one with timber frame upon a stone bas
emphasising Weston Subedge's position on the borde
between Cotswold hills and Evesham vale. The churc
is at the upper end of the village, looking up toward
the hills. The prettily pinnacled tower is Perpendicula
but the rest of the church is heavily Victorianised
However do not miss the handsome late Jacobea
pulpit, nor the brass to William Hodges.....a very sma
Elizabethan gentleman.

Stone and Thatch, Stanway

MAP 10

50

WILLERSEY

(10—NE) (1½ miles North East of Broadway)
Sits astride the A 46, with wide greens either side of
the road running towards the steep Cotswold scarp.
The pleasant little Bell Inn looks across to Pool House,
with its stone gate pillars standing handsomely above
the village pond. Opposite this pond there is a quiet
cul-de-sac leading to the church, which lies on the
eastern edge of the village looking up and across to
Saintbury spire. It has a Perpendicular tower, with
pinnacles and gargoyles, and inside, below the tower,
there is fine stone vaulting (although surprisingly
enough this is mid 19th century work and not
medieval). We also liked the little 13th century north
porch, the pleasantly shaped Norman tub font, and
the Royal Arms of George III.

Pool House, Willersey

WOOD STANWAY

(10—SW) (3 miles North East of Winchcombe)
Hamlet with several beautiful houses and farms, and a
pleasant path to Stumps Cross at the top of Stanway
Hill.

MAP 4 continued from P 21.

At Wood Stanway

WESTONBIRT ARBORETUM

(To South of Map 4) (3 miles South West of Tetbury)
The magnificent Victorian mansion is now a girls school, but
we have included Westonbirt because of its splendid
arboretum. This world famous collection of trees covers 116
acres, and includes a vast variety of different species in
carefully contrived harmony, with rhododendrons, maples,
azaleas and camellias in glorious profusion. Do not miss a
visit to the 'Silk Wood', a very extensive area of semi-
ornamental woodland lying to the immediate south-west of
the car park.

WOODCHESTER

(4—NW) (2 miles North of Nailsworth)
This sits on the steep western slopes of Avon valley, linking
Stroud and Nailsworth, and there are several 18th and 19th
century mills in the valley bottom. The Victorian church
contains a few monuments taken from the old church, but
it is the churchyard where the older building stood, that
contains Woodchester's great treasure.....The Woodchester
Roman Pavement (See below).

At Westonbirt Arboretum   *Westonbirt church*

WOODCHESTER ROMAN PAVEMENT

(4—NW) (2 miles North of Nailsworth)
This is a splendid mosaic pavement, part of a large
Roman villa, first systematically excavated in 1796. It
usually lies buried in the old churchyard, but in recent
times it has usually been uncovered for one summer
every ten years. It is now possible that it will be taken
into the care of the Department of the Environment,
and that this may lead to some form of permanent
display. However this may not come to fruition for
some years.

Woodchester Roman Pavement

MAP 10

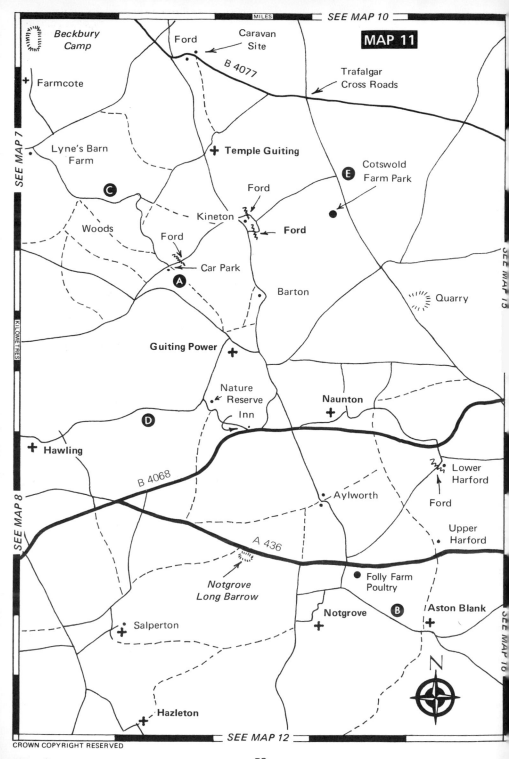

Beckbury
Camp

Ford

Caravan
Site

MAP 11

B 4077

Trafalgar
Cross Roads

Farmcote

Lyne's Barn
Farm

✚ **Temple Guiting**

C

E Cotswold
Farm Park

Ford

Woods

Kineton

Ford

Ford

Ford

Car Park

A

Barton

SEE MAP 13

Quarry

Guiting Power ✚

KILOMETRES

Nature
Reserve
Inn

Naunton
✚

D

✚ **Hawling**

B 4068

Lower
Harford

Ford

Aylworth

A 436

Upper
Harford

Notgrove
Long Barrow

Folly Farm
Poultry

Salperton

Notgrove
✚

B

Aston Blank
✚

SEE MAP 10

N

✚ **Hazleton**

CROWN COPYRIGHT RESERVED

Map II

Quiet Woodlands and the Stripling Windrush

ASTON BLANK, THE GUITINGS, NAUNTON, NOTGROVE, etc. . . .

ASTON BLANK
Sometimes referred to as **COLD ASTON**)
(11—SE) (4 miles North of Northleach)
This is a high wold village, set amidst typically rolling Cotswold country, with dry stone walls curving over the landscape, separating sheep pastures and great acreages of barley. It is centred upon a large sycamore tree on its green, which is itself overlooked by handsome Georgian Sycamore House, and the low built Plough Inn on the other side. The largely Norman church has a very plain exterior, but once inside the Norman south door, we found pleasant stone vaulting beneath the tower, a colourful 17th century monument complete with cherubs, and the remnants of a 14th century stone reredos in the east wall.

Sycamore House, Aston Blank

AYLWORTH
(11—SE) (5½ miles South West of Stow-on-the-Wold)
Quiet hamlet in an open valley with a pleasant 17th and 18th century farmhouse.

BARTON
(11—NE) (5½ miles West of Stow-on-the-Wold)
Minute hamlet with a delightful 18th century house overlooking a pool through which the infant Windrush flows on its way south to Naunton.

BECKBURY CAMP
(11—NW) (3 miles North East of Winchcombe)
Large Iron Age hill fort just to the north of Farmcote, with splendid views out over Hailes Abbey towards Bredon Hill and the distant Malverns.

Wold Country near Aston Blank — Map Ref. **B**

COTSWOLD FARM PARK
(11—NE) (5 miles West of Stow-on-the-Wold)
A unique collection of rare breeds of British farm livestock displayed in a beautiful farm setting high on the top of the Cotswolds, with pets and baby animals on show for the benefit of younger children. Breeds exhibited include Longhorn cattle, Soay and Orkney sheep, and shire horses. There is a free car park and picnic site.

FARMCOTE
(11—NW) (2 miles East of Winchcombe)
Hamlet which is (unusually) perched on the very edge of the Cotswold scarp, with mouth watering views out over the valley towards Bredon and the Malverns. There is a charming little church (a chapel of ease, to be

Aylworth

53

MAP II

Guiting Power

In Guiting Wood — Map Ref. ●

Near Hawling — Map Ref. ●

Hazleton Church

ecclesiastically correct), which looks heavily restored outside, and whose delightfully unspoilt interior therefore comes as a considerable surprise. It is a simple Norman building with a long vanished chancel. See especially the two-decker Jacobean pulpit and altar rail, the 16th century benches and the handsomely canopied tomb of Henry and Mary Stratford, in unpainted, pale stone.

There is a pleasant bridle-way down to Hailes Abbey, from which a path branches off right to Beckbury Camp after a few hundred yards.

FORD

(11—NW) (4 miles East of Winchcombe)
Small hamlet on the slopes of the upper Windrush valley, rather over-powered by the lorries and repair yards of a large haulage firm. However there is a hospitable inn, the Plough, which has an oft quoted verse on a board above its door exhorting 'ye weary travellers.....to step in and quaff my nut-brown ale' (please read in full.....it's all good stuff. There is a caravan site opposite.

GUITING POWER

(11—NW) (5 miles South East of Winchcombe)
There is evidence of much re-building in the church here, but the fine Norman doorways make a visit well worthwhile. The village is built around a smooth sloping green and is a fascinating example of the unconscious harmony created by Cotswold masons over the centuries. Here the cottages, shops and Inn are all cared for with a real understanding for their Cotswold surroundings. Ye Olde Inne, which lies away from the centre of the village offers a variety of well cooked 'bar food'.

GUITING WOOD

(11—NW) (3 miles East of Winchcombe)
Extensive woodlands bordering upon the valley of the little Castlett stream. They may be approached from Guiting Power, Kineton, Temple Guiting or Farmcote. There is a road through the valley itself, and although it is narrow and marked 'Unsuitable for Motors', it is reasonably well surfaced and should prove a practical means of access for those who cannot walk. However do drive slowly and give no offence to walkers, riders or any other road users.

Despite what we say above, we would suggest that if possible, you stop at the small car park kindly provided Ⓐ and explore the area on foot.....it is an infinitely more enjoyable and less offensive way of looking at this delightful area.

HAWLING

(11—SW) (4 miles South East of Winchcombe)
An unspoilt village in high sheep country, with a fine Elizabethan manor house next door to its church. This was re-built in 1764, and was probably in such good order in the 19th century, that it escaped the more ruthless 'restorations' of many of its fellows. We liked the Georgian pulpit, the colourful little ceiling beneath the tower, and the unusual set of 17th century brass plaques to members of the Stratford family.

HAZLETON

(11—SW) (2½ miles North West of Northleach)
A quiet village high up in the wolds with a fine bridle-

MAP 11   54

...ad across to Turkdean (P 59) and on to Aston Blank (P ...3). The church has a Norman south doorway and a massive ...3th century font. Do not miss a visit to **Folly Farm** a fine ...ollection of rare breeds of poultry, waterfowl and wildfowl ...an attractive setting, just off the A436 to the NE of the ...llage.

...INETON

(11—NW) (5 miles East of Winchcombe)
...hamlet whose charms lie mainly in the two fords ...hich cross the little tree lined Windrush, flowing ...outhwards from its source above the village of ...utsdean about three miles away. There is a pleasant ...onnington Brewery inn here, The Half Way House.

...OWER HARFORD

(11—SE) (4 miles South West of Stow-on-the-Wold)
...pleasant ford immediately beyond a neat farm-...ouse. There is a road south west towards Notgrove, ...ut the ford can be rather deep at times, and we would ...uggest that you use this route for walking rather than ...otoring.

...AUNTON

(11—SE) (5 miles West of Stow-on-the-Wold)
...ong thin village spread out along the floor of the ...eep Windrush valley, and looking like a model from ...he main road above. The church has a handsome ...erpendicular tower with pinnacles and gargoyles, and ...lthough time has not dealt as kindly as it might with ...he interior, it has a beautifully carved early 15th ...century stone pulpit, an interesting font of the same ...eriod. Do not miss the hospitable Black Horse Inn ...Donnington Ales), nor the charming 17th century ...ovecot overlooking the stream.

...IOTGROVE

(11—SE) (3 miles North of Northleach)
...nother high upland village, this one spreads thinly ...round a rough green, with church and re-built manor ...ouse at its southern edge, at the end of a drive-way ...vith pollarded trees. The stone spired, largely Norman ...hurch has a primitive Saxon crucifix on its outside ...ast wall, and its interior contains a large monument to ...nembers of the Whittington family, the descendants ...f Sir Richard (Dick) Whittington.

...IOTGROVE LONG BARROW

(11—SW) (4 miles North of Northleach)
...lost of the earth covering the stone burial chambers ...f this Stone Age long barrow has been removed long ...go, and the massive stones that remain, give some idea ...f what the gallery and burial chambers must have ...nce looked like. However for prehistoric flavour we ...refer Belas Knap or Hetty Pegler's Tump.
There is an attractive bridle-way from here to ...alperton.

...ALPERTON

(11—SW) (4 miles North West of Northleach)
...alperton Park is a 17th century manor house, much ...ltered in the 19th century. The adjoining church has a ...ate Norman chancel arch, and there is a fascinating ...nedieval wall painting of a skeleton with scythe and ...rrow.....'Old Father Time' perhaps? Salperton Park is ...rivate property, but there is a public path to the ...hurch in front of the house.

...EMPLE GUITING see P 87.

*'Cotswold Perspective', near Kineton —
Map Ref.* ❺

Ford at Lower Harford

Naunton

*Saxon Carving,
Notgrove*

*Salperton Manor,
from the church porch*

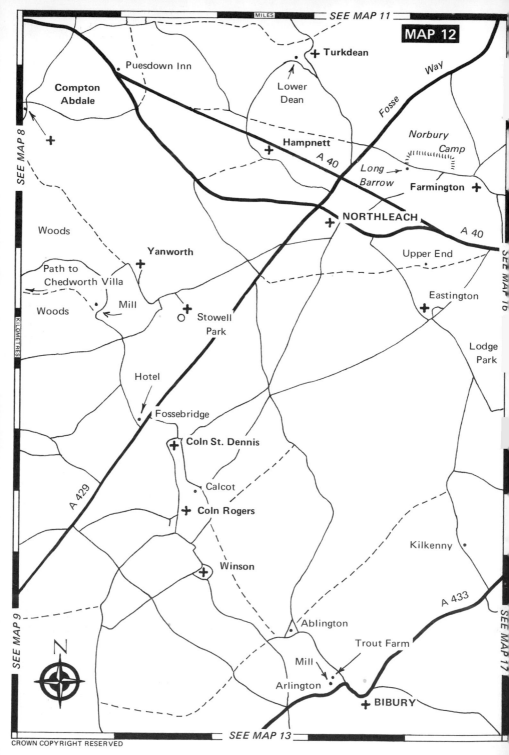

MILES

MAP 12

Turkdean

Puesdown Inn

Compton
Abdale

Lower
Dean

Fosse Way

Norbury
Camp

Hampnett

A 40

Long
Barrow

Farmington

NORTHLEACH

A 40

Woods

Upper End

Yanworth

Eastington

Path to
Chedworth Villa

Lodge
Park

Woods

Mill

Stowell
Park

KILOMETRES

Hotel

Fossebridge

Coln St. Dennis

A 429

Calcot

Coln Rogers

Kilkenny

Winson

A 433

Ablington

Trout Farm

Mill

Arlington

BIBURY

Map 12

Fosse Country and the Middle Coln

BIBURY, COLN ROGERS, COLN ST. DENNIS, NORTHLEACH, etc. . . .

ABLINGTON

(12—SE) (1 mile North West of Bibury)
Mouth-watering hamlet on the Coln, a short distance upstream from Bibury, with a fine 16th century manor house, and Ablington House, a beautiful 17th century building complete with lions, which once graced the Houses of Parliament, upon its gateposts. It would be difficult to overlook the two splendid barns (one dated 1727) near the middle of the hamlet.

ARLINGTON See Bibury below.

BIBURY (and ARLINGTON)

(12—SE) (6 miles North East of Cirencester)
This village can become crowded at holiday times, but its popularity is well deserved and its inhabitants have resisted the temptation to over commercialise. If poss ible park near the bridge across from the Swan Hotel, visit the Trout Farm and Arlington Mill Museum, and then walk along the far side of Rack Isle, where wool once dried after being washed in Arlington Row, a delightful row of cottages, which like Rack Isle, are in the care of the National Trust. Pass Arlington Row and then cross the stream, pausing of course to gaze downwards at the trout gliding translucently by, quite undeterred by noisy ducks and moorhens; and then walk down to the fascinating church. This building standing in a trim churchyard with cherub table tombs and fragrant rose trees, dates back to Anglo Saxon times (see the chancel arch jambs and joints, and the fragments of a cross shaft). There are also Norman north and south doorways, the latter within a Norman porch.

CALCOT

(12—SW) (2½ miles North West of Bibury)
A quiet hamlet on the eastern slopes of the Coln valley, with several pleasant cottages lining its single street.

COLN ROGERS

(12—SW) (2½ miles North West of Bibury)
The Coln valley is broad here, and there are woods on the far side above the stream, looking back to the Saxon church, which is tucked well away from the road. Much of the original Saxon nave and chancel remain.....see especially the chancel arch and one of the windows in the north side, made out of a single block of stone, the beautifully simple 15th century stone pulpit, and the tomb recess with the little medieval head stops.

Barn at Ablington

The Swan Hotel, Bibury

Coln Rogers Church

Pulpit at Coln Rogers

COLN ST. DENNIS

(12—SW) (3 miles North West of Bibury)
Another attractive village, with a tall towered Norman church looking out across the Coln water meadows. Apart from its top, even the central tower is Norman and the Norman west tower arch, although under great stress, still survives (the east tower arch had to be re built when the 15th century tower top was added). Do not miss the weird collection of Norman corbel figures supporting the nave roof.

Coln St. Dennis Church

North Porch,
Compton Abdale

Crocodile at
Compton Abdale

COMPTON ABDALE

(12—NW) (3 miles West of Northleach)
Small village in a deep valley, with a church built into a steep bank overlooking the cross roads. It has a finely pinnacled and gargoyled Perpendicular tower, but the interior has been over-restored. Our favourite curiosity here is the little stone 'crocodile' below the church yard, from which a stream gushes out and flows down the roadside.

EASTINGTON

(12—NE) (1 mile South East of Northleach)
Hamlet in a bowl-like setting in the wolds, with the little River Leach flowing beside the road. There are fine barns and a small mid-Victorian chapel on a slope overlooking the valley. At Upper End, half a mile to the north east, there is a fine 15th century manor house and a circular dovecot.

FARMINGTON

(12—NE) (1½ miles North East of Northleach)
Small village on high ground between the Leach and Sherborne valleys, with a large green, on which stands a little octagonal pumphouse. Farmington Lodge is partly 18th and partly 19th century, and has four massive Doric columns gracing its front.....all rather grand for little Farmington. The church which lies across the road from the Lodge, is a largely Norman building, with Norman south doorway, chancel arch and north aisle arcade. The well proportioned tower was added in the 15th century.

Norbury Camp lies to the east of the village, and is an Iron Age hill fort, with a Stone Age long barrow within its earthworks (south west corner).

On the Green at Farmington

FOSSEBRIDGE

(12—SW) (3 miles South West of Northleach)
Hamlet marking the point where the Fosse Way drops into a deep valley to cross the Coln. There is a pleasant hotel here beside the bridge.

HAMPNETT

(12—NE) (1 mile North West of Northleach)
An attractive village spread thinly around a field-like village green, which gives birth to one of the Cotswold's most beautiful streams.....the River Leach. The church is largely Norman, but its interior was subjected to some very unusual stencil decoration in the 1880's. This detracts from the clean Norman lines, although most churches in the Middle Ages were decorated with a variety of 'all over' patterns similar to this. Note the finely carved birds on the capitals supporting the chancel arch.

Norman Birds at Hampnett

MAP 12   58

NORTHLEACH

(12—NE) (10 miles North East of Cirencester)
This was one of the most important Cotswold wool centres, and only acknowledged Chipping Campden and Cirencester as its superiors. This pleasant little town is now happily bye-passed by the busy A40 and has regained the tranquility that it enjoyed before the age of the motor car.

Its fine 'wool church' was entirely re-built in the 15th century and is a splendid example of the Perpendicular style.....see especially its wonderful tower and south porch, its stone pulpit and its fine series of wood merchant's brasses. These underline the importance of the Cotswold wool men who held a significant position not only in England but also in European trade in the Middle Ages.

Do not miss a visit to the interesting Cotswold Countryside Collection...a museum housed in an 18th century 'House of Correction', situated at the cross roads to the west of the town.

Northleach

STOWELL

(12—NW) (2 miles South West of Northleach)
A fine Elizabethan mansion in a large park, looking westwards over the Coln valley, to the Chedworth woods. Behind the mansion there is a small Norman church. This has been over restored externally, but the interior is full of character and contains some fascinating and very early 'Doom' wall paintings, which must have been executed soon after the church was built 1150—1200). The church lies within the bounds of the estate and we suggest that you walk up the drive from the Northleach—Yanworth road). Parking on the roadside is a problem, but the probably long walk will be well justified.

Wall Painting, Stowell

TURKDEAN

(12—NE) (2 miles North of Northleach)
Pleasantly sited on a hillside, with the hamlet of Lower Dean in the valley below, the two parts being joined by road leading through a magnificent avenue of beech trees. The Norman church has some interesting items of early sculpture, a pleasing Perpendicular north doorway and porch, and a large 15th century stone pulpit. Do not overlook the interesting photograph of the vaulted undercroft (or crypt) of nearby Rectory Farm.

There is an interesting bridle road over to Aston Blank and also one to Hazleton.

Below Winson Church

WINSON

(12—SW) (2 miles North West of Bibury)
Small village on the Coln, with a little Norman church poised above a typically beautiful group of farm buildings, with some 18th century table tombs in its neat churchyard. It has a Norman south doorway and chancel arch, and a 15th century stone pulpit, although the altar has been drastically over-restored.

YANWORTH

(12—NW) (2 miles West of Northleach)
A small village overlooking the Coln valley. The little Norman church lies amongst a noble group of farm buildings a short distance from the village. Do not miss the wall painting of Old Father Time complete with his scythe.

Mill House between Winson and Coln Rogers

MAP 12

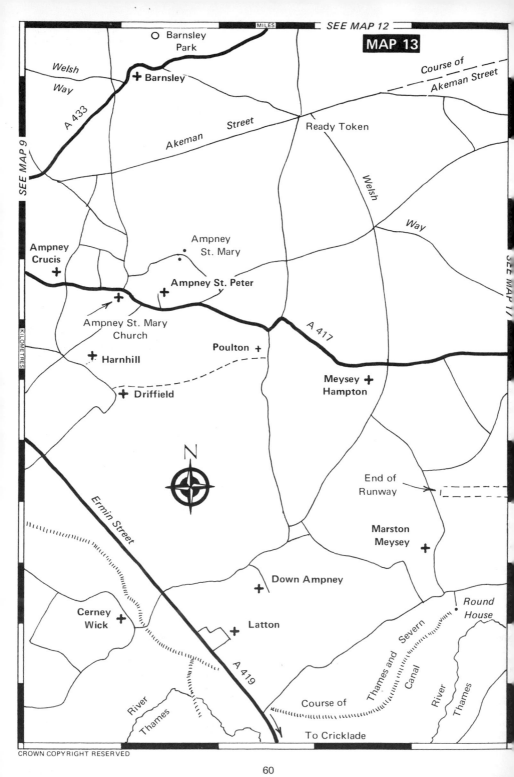

MILES

O Barnsley
Park

Welsh
Way

✝ Barnsley

A 433

Course of
Akeman Street

Akeman Street

Ready Token

Welsh

Way

Ampney
St. Mary

Ampney
Crucis
✝

✝ Ampney St. Peter

Ampney St. Mary
Church
✝

✝ Harnhill

Poulton ✝

A 417

✝ Driffield

Meysey ✝
Hampton

KILOMETRES

N

End of
Runway

Ermin Street

Marston
Meysey ✝

Round
House

Cerney
Wick ✝

Down Ampney
✝

✝ Latton

Thames and Severn Canal

River
Thames

A 419

River
Thames

River
Thames

Course of

To Cricklade

Map 13

Southwards to the Thames

THE AMPNEYS, BARNSLEY, CRICKLADE and the MEYSEYS

AKEMAN STREET

(Maps 13–17–20–23–26)
An important Roman road which ran from Cirencester to Bicester, and onwards to St. Albans. Unlike many Roman roads, it has not been retained as a part of our main road network, although several sections in the southern Cotswolds are used as minor roads, and a few as bridle-ways and foot-paths.

AMPNEY CRUCIS

(13–NW) (2 miles East of Cirencester)
Has a dclapidated water mill, and beyond; a beautiful church tucked away beneath the wall of Ampney Park. In the churchyard is a remarkably well preserved 14th century cross, whose head was only re-discovered in 1854, built-up in the rood loft stair. See also the splendid 16th century tomb of George and Annie Lloyd, the rare stone Perpendicular pulpit, and behind it, a door leading to the rood loft stair.

Ampney Crucis Church

AMPNEY ST. MARY

(13–NW) (4 miles East of Cirencester)
A small village, unexceptional apart from its church which lies almost a mile to the south west, just beyond the A 417 and beside the little Ampney Brook. This is a small Norman building with pleasant 'Decorated' style windows, all of which was lightly restored in 1913. See especially the fascinating Norman lintel over the north doorway, the medieval south door, the stone chancel screen and the extensive series of medieval wall paintings.

Effigy at Ampney Crucis

AMPNEY ST. PETER

(13–NW) (3½ miles East of Cirencester)
Small village to the immediate north of the A 417, with a little freehouse full of character, called the Packhorse Inn, and several very well restored houses and cottages... all perhaps a little too trim. The church has a Saxon nave, but the restoration and re-building by Sir Giles Gilbert Scott in 1878 has left little sense of antiquity here. However do not miss the primitive little figure just inside the door, nor the remains of a 14th century cross in the churchyard.

BARNSLEY

(13–NW) (4 miles North East of Cirencester)
The main road traffic spoils an otherwise attractive village of small neat houses and gardens. The largely Norman church has a tower whose top was built as late

Barnsley Church

MAP 13

Cricklade Church

South Porch, Down Ampney

Monuments at Down Ampney

as the early 17th century. Do not miss the very early Norman window, in the organ chamber hewn out of a single stone, which was moved here from Daglingworth. Other re-building work was carried out here by Sir Edmund Tame of Fairford (see Fairford, P 80 and Rendcomb, P 45).

The 'Village Pub' has a welcoming 'Buttery Bar', and is a pleasant place to stop awhile. The delightful gardens of Barnsley House, on the main road, are open at certain times during the summer. The fine Georgian mansion of Barnsley Park lies to the north of the village, and is just visible from the road to Bibury.

CERNEY WICK

(13—SW) (5 miles South East of Cirencester) Small village in the flat Thames gravel country, with large flooded pits to the west and the line of the old Thames and Severn Canal to the immediate east. There is a small Victorian church and yet another 'Round House' with 18th century Gothick windows, built for the canal maintenance men. The River Churn flows through Cerney Wick on its way to join the Thames about a mile to the south east.

CRICKLADE

(Just South of Map 13)
(7 miles South East of Cirencester) Cricklade is dominated by the proud 16th century tower of St. Samson's church, and the traffic that perpetually thunders down the Ermin Street. St. Samsons' has massive arcading, and impressive vaulting beneath its tower, but we preferred the smaller and simpler interior of St. Mary's. This has an excellent Norman chancel arch and an attractive timbered roof with traceried bordering. In fact, St. Mary's has the charm and dignity of the poor relation, and should not be missed.

DOWN AMPNEY

(13—SE) (5 miles South East of Cirencester) Vaughan Williams, the composer, was born here in 1872, the son of the vicar. It is a long straggling village in flat country only about two miles away from the Thames, with only two buildings of real interest both of which lie quietly amongst trees at its southern end. The cruciform church has a fine 14th century spire and a large 15th century porch. The interior was richly (and heavily) restored at the turn of the century. However do not miss the effigies of a knight in black marble and a lady in stone in the south transept, the 17th century monument to the two Hungerford knights in the north transept, acting as a reredos, nor the excellent copy of Giorgione's 'Madonna of Castel Franco'.

Beside the church stands Down Ampney House, a handsome 15th century manor, embellished by Sir John Soane in 1799.

DRIFFIELD

(13—SW) (3 miles East of Cirencester) Small village with pleasantly noisy duck pond (the ducks make a refreshing change from the aircraft of South Cerney), and a church which was re-built in 1734 and heavily restored in 1863, almost certainly by that redoubtable Victorian architect, William Butterfield. Do not miss the inscription to George Hanger, Lord Coleraine, whose gambling debts were almost certainly responsible for the high walled garden next to the church. (For this was part of a mansion, sold to pay his debts, and then demolished.)

MAP 13   62

HARNHILL

(13–NW) (2½ miles East of Cirencester)
Compact village with a little Norman church standing almost in the garden of the largely Georgian rectory. Its chief treasure is the Norman south doorway's tympanum, with St. Michael fighting a dragon, but there are also lovely fragments of medieval glass in the east window. This church escaped the Victorians and was most sympathetically restored in 1909.

Also near the church is a 16th century manor house, with a beautiful square dovecot in its grounds.

LATTON

(13–SW) (1½ miles North West of Cricklade)
Lies in water meadow country near the union of the Churn with the Thames, with another Round House (see Cerney Wick P 62) close by. The stout Norman church was heavily restored by William Butterfield in 1861, and lacks atmosphere. However there are pleasant stone floors and an amusing series of corbel figures in the nave.

MARSTON MEYSEY

(13–SE) (3 miles South West of Fairford)
A long thin village in flat country not far from the monstrous runway of Fairford airfield, where the Concorde was based during its flight testing. The church is Victorian and not of great interest to visitors, but there are many lovely old tombs in the churchyard. There is a canal Round House (see Cerney Wick P 62) reached by a pleasant footpath leading from here across water meadows to Castle Eaton, on the Thames.

MEYSEY HAMPTON

(13–SE) (2 miles West of Fairford)
A very trim village with a semi-circular green overlooked by the Mason's Arms and a fine Georgian manor house. The 13th century cruciform church was probably built by the Knights Templar. Like the village it is a neat, trim building, and has four well sculptured tower arches. Do not overlook the handsome three seater sedilia with a piscina in a fourth niche, nor the very engaging 17th century monument to James Vaulx (1626) with his two wives.

POULTON

(13–NW) (3 miles West of Fairford)
An unexceptional village in flat country with a modest little inn, the Falcon, overlooked by an equally modest late 17th century manor house across the road. The church and school were both built by William Butterfield, and having viewed the large bare interior, one can only lament the passing of the little church that it replaced (there is a water colour of it hanging in Butterfield's church).

THE WELSH WAY

(13–NW.....etc.)
There are several of these drove roads across the Cotswolds, used by the Welsh cattle drovers to bring their beasts to the London markets before the coming of the railways. The Welsh Way, westwards from Barnsley was probably a prehistoric trackway before it was used by the drovers, and it certainly provides a pleasant contrast to the busy A 417 as it winds across country towards the Fosse Way.

Latton Church

Cherubs at Marston Meysey

Round House near Marston Meysey

Vaulx Monument, Meysey Hampton

63

MAP 13

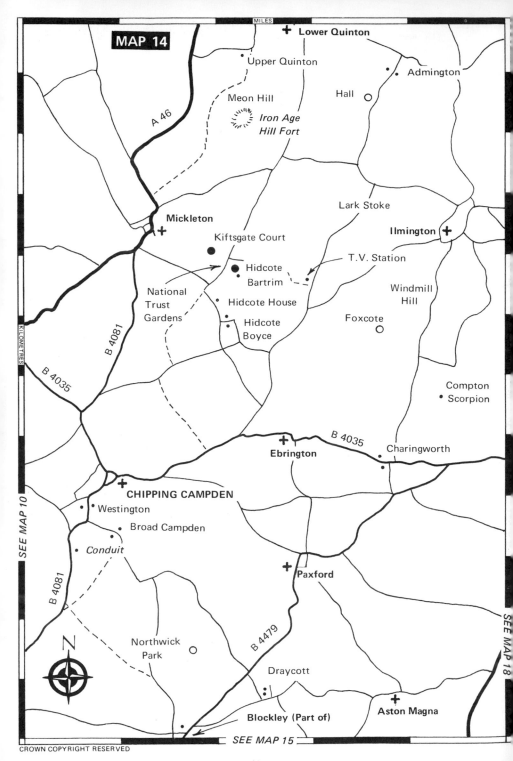

MILES

MAP 14

Lower Quinton

Upper Quinton

Admington

Hall

Meon Hill

Iron Age
Hill Fort

A 46

Lark Stoke

Mickleton

Ilmington

Kiftsgate Court

T.V. Station

Hidcote
Bartrim

Windmill
Hill

National
Trust
Gardens

Hidcote House

Foxcote

B 4081

Hidcote
Boyce

B 4035

Compton
Scorpion

B 4035

Ebrington

Charingworth

CHIPPING CAMPDEN

Westington

Broad Campden

Paxford

Conduit

B 4081

Northwick
Park

B 4479

Draycott

Blockley (Part of)

Aston Magna

SEE MAP 15

N

Map 14

Chipping Campden and the Far North

CHIPPING CAMPDEN, EBRINGTON, HIDCOTE GARDENS, ILMINGTON, etc. . . .

ADMINGTON

(14–NE) (5 miles North East of Chipping Campden) An unexceptional hamlet lying in valley country to the north of Ilmington Downs and relieved only by Admington Hall, a pleasant 17th century mansion with an 18th century front.

ASTON MAGNA

(14–SE) (3½ miles South East of Chipping Campden) Lying on the slopes of a hill looking towards the Stour valley, his village has a few pleasant stone houses and barns, and a little green, on which stands the base and lower part of a medieval cross. The circular earthworks to the south of the church are thought to be the remains of a medieval 'Homestead Moat', the landlords of which were the Bishops of Worcester.

High Street, Chipping Campden

BROAD CAMPDEN

(14–SW) (1 mile South of Chipping Campden) Small village with a little Victorian church and an 18th century Quaker meeting house. There is also a house converted from a Norman chapel by C. R. Ashbee, the founder of the 'Guild of Handicrafts', which he moved from London to Campden in 1902.

CHARINGWORTH

(14–SE) (3 miles East of Chipping Campden) Hamlet with manor house and farms, all looking southwards from orchard covered hillsides. There is a pleasant open road north from here over Windmill Hill, and steeply down to Ilmington.

Market Hall, Chipping Campden

CHIPPING CAMPDEN

(14 -SW) (5 miles North West of Moreton-in-Marsh) This is without doubt the finest of the Cotswold Wool Towns. It was at the height of its prosperity in the later Middle Ages, when Cotswold Wool was famous throughout Western Europe. Unlike several other towns of equal beauty, it has aged gracefully, and although the visitor is catered for, the town has avoided most of the pitfalls of modern tourism.

Almost every house in Campden's High Street is worth looking at. Cotswold Masons, working with the local stone have given their own unique flavour to the whole run of architectural styles, from the Gothic magnificence of Grevel's House to the classical dignity of Bedfont House.

The charming little Woolstaplers Hall Museum should on no account be missed.

Chipping Campden Church

MAP 14

Ebrington

Hidcote House, Hidcote Boyce

Hidcote Manor Gardens

Cottage at Hidcote Boyce

Ilmington Church

DRAYCOTT

(14—SE) (3 miles South East of Chipping Campden)
A quiet hamlet in a broad valley to the north east of
Blockley (P 69), with a pleasant row of cottages leading to a small 18th century farmhouse. There is a small
factory nearby, producing glass fibre sailing craft.

EBRINGTON

(14—SE) (2 miles East of Chipping Campden)
Attractive village, still known to many locals as
Yubberton; with a road lined with thatched stone
cottages leading to its centre, which is overlooked by a
war memorial and the beautifully signed Ebrington
Arms. What a pity that so many overhead wires and
road signs are in evidence.

The church lies above most of the village and has a
good solid tower and a Norman south doorway with
geometric design upon its tympanum. The interior has
been over restored, but we liked the monument to
Lord Chief Justice Sir John Fortesque (1476), the two
Keyte monuments, and the notice reading.....William
Keyte Esq., A.D. 1632 left by will the milk of ten good
and sufficent milch kine to the poor of Ebrington
from May 10th—November 1st for ever'. However a
note at the bottom reads, 'This charge was redeemed
1952'. What a shame!

HIDCOTE BARTRIM

(14—NW) (3 miles North East of Chipping Campden)
A few pleasant cottages and a farm, situated just
beyond Hidcote Manor (see below), make up this small
hamlet below Lark Stoke Hill. The gardens of Kiftsgate
Court are open to the public at certain times.

HIDCOTE BOYCE

(14—NW) (2 miles North East of Chipping Campden)
Agreeable hamlet with a gently sloping street bordered
by flower filled cottage gardens. Hidcote House is an
exquisite 17th century manor, with beautifully shaped
gable ends and ever present fan-tail doves.

HIDCOTE MANOR GARDENS, HIDCOTE BARTRIM

(14—NW) (3 miles North East of Chipping Campden)
Given to the National Trust in 1948 by Lawrence
Johnson, who had spent over forty years on its creation. Hidcote's subtle design embraces a series of small
gardens, through which the visitor is drawn onward
by ever changing vistas beyond. Many of the gardens
are surrounded by magnificent hedges and there are
pools, mellow brick gazebos and wrought iron gates
through which one can glimpse distant views of the
Avon valley and Bredon Hill.

Hidcote Garden is a highly satisfying place to visit
and will delight all who come this way..... Do not miss
it, please.

ILMINGTON

(14—NE) (5 miles North East of Chipping Campden)
A widespread but exceedingly pleasant village at the
foot of Ilmington Downs. Ilmington has a wealth of
attractive old houses and cottages, which have grouped
over the years into unplanned perfection.

Leave your car and walk up the quiet back road
and footpaths to visit the church, an interesting Norman structure with a fine 16th century porch. Inside

MAP 14　　　　　66

will be found the splendid oak furnishings of Robert Thompson, of Kilburn in Yorkshire, noted for the carvings of a mouse to be found on each of his works. Can you find his eleven mice here?

LARK STOKE HILL
(14—NE) (2½ miles North East of Chipping Campden) At 850 feet above sea level, this is the highest point in Warwickshire, and one of the northern bastions of the Cotswolds. Despite the small T.V. transmitter, this is still good walking country, with a track up from Hidcote Gardens, joining at the transmitter, a track leading over the hill and down northwards to meet the Ilmington—Mickleton road. Inevitably there are splendid views out over the Avon valley and beyond to the Midland Plain.

Meon Hill

MEON HILL
(14—NW) (1½ miles North East of Mickleton) There is an Iron Age hill fort on the top of this outlier of the Cotswolds dominating the Avon valley. There are fine views and persistent rumours of witchcraft. Much of the area is usually under cultivation, but the south-western slopes are often the scene of hang-gliding on Sundays, and this can usually be watched from the Ilmington road.

MICKLETON
(14—NW) (3 miles North of Chipping Campden) Large village beneath the Cotswold edge, with much modern development on its fringes. However there are many pleasant houses and cottages, some of stone, some half-timbered, within the confines of the old village and despite the A 46's traffic, Mickleton has retained considerable character. See especially the lovely 'Cotswold-Queen Anne' style Medford House, and the little Victorian 'Memorial Fountain' by the Three Ways Hotel.
The church lies on the edge of the village, looking up to the hills, and there is a pleasant walk up from here to Hidcote Manor Gardens (P 66). It has a fine 14th century tower and spire, a handsome and most unusual 17th century porch, and within, a 12th century crucifix or rood (over the north aisle chapel altar).

Church Porch, Mickleton

NORTHWICK PARK
(14—SW) (2 miles South of Chipping Campden) Large 17th and 18th century mansion in a great park It is not properly visible from the road, nor is it open to the public.

QUINTON
(14—NW) (2 miles North East of Mickleton) Attractive village whose 130 foot church spire dominates one or two lovely old houses, several thatched black and white cottages, and a well restored inn, the College Arms. The church has a Norman south arcade and a Norman font, but the tomb of Sir William Clopton and his wife would by itself justify a look inside this most pleasing building.

Memorial Fountain, Mickleton

WESTINGTON
(14—SW) (To immediate South of Chipping Campden) Quiet part of Chipping Campden, with many lovely old houses and cottages, several of which are thatched. On Westington Hill, to its south, is a little conduit built beside the road in 1612, to supply water to the almshouses by Campden church.

The College Arms, Quinton

MAP 14

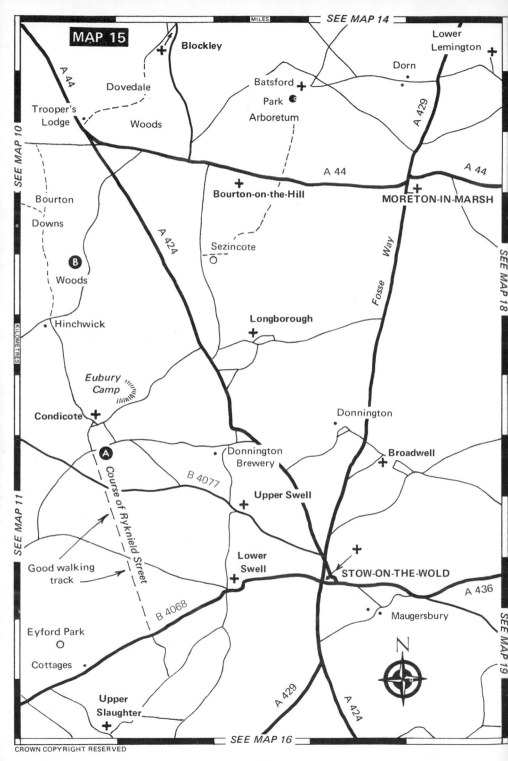

MAP 15

SEE MAP 14

MILES

Blockley

Lower
Lemington

A 44

Dovedale

Dorn

Batsford
Park
Arboretum

Trooper's
Lodge

Woods

A 429

SEE MAP 10

A 44

A 44

Bourton-on-the-Hill

MORETON-IN-MARSH

Bourton
Downs

A 424

Sezincote

SEE MAP 18

B

Woods

Hinchwick

Fosse Way

Longborough

Eubury
Camp

Donnington

Condicote

A

Donnington
Brewery

Broadwell

B 4077

Upper Swell

SEE MAP 11

Course of Ryknield Street

Good walking
track

Lower
Swell

STOW-ON-THE-WOLD

A 436

B 4068

Maugersbury

SEE MAP 19

Eyford Park

O

Cottages

N

Upper
Slaughter

A 429

A 424

SEE MAP 16

CROWN COPYRIGHT RESERVED

Map 15

High Wolds and a Delectable Brewery

BLOCKLEY, MORETON-IN-MARSH, STOW-ON-THE-WOLD, THE SWELLS, UPPER SLAUGHTER, etc....

BATSFORD

(15—NE) (1½ miles North West of Moreton-in-Marsh)
Tidy little estate village, at the gates of Batsford Park, a late 19th century Tudor mansion, which has a fine arboretum with trees and shrubs, and a Chinese temple (Arboretum access from A44...See Map opposite). The church is an ambitious Victorian building with tall spire and apsidal chancel, and is worth visiting for the sake of the handsome tablet to Thomas Edward Freeman (1808) by the sculptor Joseph Nollekens.

BLOCKLEY

(15—NW) (3 miles North West of Moreton-in-Marsh)
A large village built on the steep slopes of a hollow beneath the high wolds, and utterly unspoilt by tourism. Blockley's steep streets and terraces are full of character, with 17th and 18th century houses accompanied by many dignified 19th century buildings. This was the result of Blockley's prosperity as a silk centre, and at one time there were no fewer than six mills employing in all well over five hundred people (see the old mill beyond its pool below the church). Although the railway never came nearer than Paxford, there is a small inn, still proudly entitled the Great Western Arms.

The church has a Norman chancel, which was probably once vaulted, and a tower built as late as 1725 in the Gothic style. There is a large airy interior, with plenty of plain glass and a flat ceiling. See especialy the Jacobean pulpit, the series of elaborate monuments to the various owners of Northwick Park, and the two brasses, both of priests.....one in the chancel floor, and one (unusually) in the centre of a sedilia.

Don't miss Blockley. The medieval Bishops of Worcester chose wisely, when they made their summer residence here.

BOURTON-ON-THE-HILL

(15—NW) (2 miles West of Moreton-in-Marsh)
Apart from noise from the steep and busy A 44, on which it all lies, everything is a delight at Bourton-on-the-Hill. At the top of the hill stands an 18th century stone built inn, the Horse and Groom; then down the road goes, past pretty terraces of 17th and 18th century cottages, past the golden stone church, to the bottom end of the village, which is enriched by elegant Bourton House, in the grounds of which stand a fine 16th century barn (dated 1570).

The church has a clerestory added in the 15th century and this, together with its handsome three stage tower, gives it a totally Perpendicular look. However

Batsford Church   *Bourton-on-the-Hill Church*

Old Silk Mill, Blockley

Terrace at Blockley

MAP 15

Condicote

Ryknield Street, South of Condicote —
Map Ref. Ⓐ

Donnington Brewery

Lake and Brewery, Donnington

once within the pleasant cream painted interior, the massive arcade columns reveal its Norman origins (the pointed arches were probably a 12th or 13th century alteration). There are stone floors and a minute 18th century gallery near the north door. The beautiful bell metal Winchester Bushel and Peck, dated 1816, are a rare survival of these English standard measures, and were used by local magistrates in the settlement of disputes (usually relating to the payment of tithes). Do not overlook the 15th century octagonal font, nor the colourful 18th century wall tablets.

BROADWELL

(15—SE) (1½ miles North East of Stow-on-the-Wold) This village is spread around its wide green beneath a hillside which rises up towards Stow-on-the-Wold. It is overlooked by a warm little inn, the Fox; and there is a small ford at its lower end. The church stands in a pleasant tree shaded churchyard, with many beautiful 17th century table tombs. It has an elegant Perpendicular tower, complete with re-set Norman tympanum over its outer turret stair entrance. Do not miss the 17th century monument, with Herbert Weston and his wife both kneeling at a prayer desk.

CONDICOTE

(15—SW) (3 miles North West of Stow-on-the-Wold) An unspoilt little upland village lying just to the east of the Ryknield Street (P 49), which provides a fine walk south south-east from here over high wold country for 2½ miles. Condicote is centred upon a large rough green encircled by a dry-stone wall, and enriched by young trees and daffodils when we last called. The green is overlooked by a 14th century wayside cross, four handsome farmhouses, and a little Norman church. Unfortunately this was ruthlessly 'restored' in 1888, and the walls have been scraped and re-pointed. However the Norman south doorway has survived, and there is an interesting little corbel figure beneath the 13th century piscina.

DONNINGTON

(15—SE) (1½ miles North of Stow-on-the-Wold) A hamlet with fine views over the Evenlode valley. It was here that Lord Astley, with 3000 Royalist troops, surrendered to the Parliamentarians on March 21st, 1646; the final defeat of the bitter Civil War.

DONNINGTON BREWERY

(15—SW) (1½ miles North West of Stow-on-the-Wold) Although not open to visitors, this must surely be Britain's most delectable brewery. The lake, or mill pond, on which it stands, is the source of the River Dickler, and its waters still turn the great mill wheel. Donnington Brewery owns a fair number of inns, all in and around the Cotswolds. It is a truly Cotswold undertaking, with these inns always appearing to add to, rather than detract from the charm of the towns and villages in which they are situated. If you appreciate real beer 'from the wood', keep an eye open for Donnington's well painting, black and white inn signs.

DOVEDALE

(15—NW) (Just South of Blockley) There is a pleasant walk from this hamlet to the immediate south of Blockley, up through Bourton Woods, to Trooper's Lodge, an attractive little 'classical' building on the main A 44.

MAP 15   70

EUBURY CAMP

(15—SW) (3 miles North West of Stow-on-the-Wold) Crescent shaped earthworks in pleasant country to the east of Condicote. Possibly the remains of an Iron Age hill fort, although its exact origins are not clear.

EYFORD PARK

(15—SW) (2½ miles West of Stow-on-the-Wold) A Queen Anne style mansion built by Sir Guy Dawber in 1910, in a fine park with a lake, near the source of the little River Eye.....the stream that has so enriched the two Slaughters (P 73, 77). None of this is visible from the A 436, but there is an attractive row of late 18th century estate cottages in the wooded valley where this road crosses the Eye. Apparently there is a tablet on a well in the park, claiming that John Milton wrote part of Paradise Lost whilst seated beside it.

Early Spring near Hinchwick — Map Ref. **B**

HINCHWICK

(15—NW) (4 miles North West of Stow-on-the-Wold) An early 19th century manor house, on the line of the Ryknield Street (P 49), at the southern end of a beautifully quiet, wooded valley, with a secret lake set deep amongst the trees. (Please do not trespass.) The attractive manor gardens have frequently been open to the public during recent years. There is a bridle-way north from here through woods, and over the wold country of Bourton Downs, from whence one can move westwards to Snowshill (P 49).

South Porch and Transept, Longborough

LONGBOROUGH

(15—NW) (2½ miles North of Stow-on-the-Wold) Attractively sited village on a hill slope looking out eastwards over the broad Evenlode valley, with a pleasant inn called the Coach and Horses (Donnington Ales), two bright little shops, many neat houses and cottages, and a medieval church, once belonging to Hailes Abbey. This has a 13th century tower, with an added upper stage, in the best Perpendicular tradition, complete with pinnacles and gargoyles. The sunken path to the south porch is overlooked by the beautiful 'Decorated' style windows of the 14th century south transept. This transept houses the very grand 17th century monument to Sir William Leigh (1631) complete with his wife and children; together with a 14th century knight and lady, for whom this transept was probably built. The north transept is sealed off, and houses the tomb of Sir Charles Cockerell (1837) of nearby Sezincote (P 72). Do not overlook the beautiful 14th century font...a tall richly sculptured piece.

Monument at Longborough

LOWER LEMINGTON

(15—NE) (1½ miles North East of Moreton-in-Marsh) A comfortable little hamlet in bumpy field country, and apparently down a private road (we suggest that you walk from the 'C' road). Houses, farm, cottages and church.....all are spread round an open field-cum-farmyard. The little church has a narrow Norman doorway within the porch, and also an exceptionally narrow Norman chancel arch. There are pleasant old Commandment Boards, but we have been deprived of any real atmosphere, by those scraping, tidy-up-everything Victorians. However do not miss a walk across to Lower Lemington, as the character of the hamlet as a whole is delightful.

Lower Lemington Church

MAP 15

South Porch, Lower Swell

House at Maugersbury

Stow Cross

LOWER SWELL

(15—SW) (1 mile West of Stow-on-the-Wold)
This suffers the disadvantage of lying on the main
Cheltenham—Stow road, but it is a tidy, well built
village with a pleasant 17th century inn called the
Golden Ball (Donnington Ales), and a small hotel. It
lies in the valley of the little River Dickler, which
flows through the park of Abbotswood, a fine early
20th century house, built by Sir Edwin Lutyens, and
at one time, the home of farm tractor millionaire
Harry Ferguson. Abbotswood gardens are particularly
lovely and may possibly be open to the public on
certain Sundays.

Lower Swell church lies to the north of the village.
The original Norman building is now the south aisle
and this contains the former Norman chancel arch
which is enriched with a splendid series of animal
carvings. The Norman south doorway is equally interesting and has a tympanum depicting a dove eating
fruit from the 'tree of life'.

MAUGERSBURY

(15—SE) (½ mile South East of Stow-on-the-Wold)
Quiet hamlet on south eastern slopes below Stow-on-
the-Wold, with pleasant views across to Icomb Hill.
There are several 17th century farmhouses, but no
features of special interest.

MORETON-IN-MARSH

(15—NE) (4 miles North of Stow-on-the-Wold)
Small town with stone built shops, houses and coaching
inns facing each other across the splendidly wide Foss
Way, and always busy with traffic between the Mid-
lands and the South West. The church, which lies away
to the east of the High Street (Fosse Way), is a
Victorian re-build of a former chapel of ease for
Bourton-on-the-Hill, and is not of great interest to
visitors. However do not overlook the little 16th century Curfew Tower, at the corner of Oxford Street, nor
the elegant 18th century house to the east of the
church. Although it has no other single feature of
special interest. Moreton has a robust charm and we
particularly favour the wide tree-lined greens at its
northern end. There are several excellent hotels.

SEZINCOTE

(15—NW) (2½ miles South West of Moreton-in-Marsh)
Sezincote provides a unique opportunity to view authentic
Mogul architecture and decoration in a rural English setting.
Built and landscaped in the first decade of the 19th century
for Sir Charles Cockerell, Bt., by his architect brother S. P.
Cockerell, with much help from Thomas Daniell, the well
known painter of Indian scenes, and from Humphrey Repton.
Sezincote was visited in 1806 by the Prince Regent who was
staying nearby. The favourable impression it then made upon
him had its effect in the subsequent Indianisation of the rebuilt
Pavilion at Brighton. Delightfully restored interior and beautiful
gardens astride the infant Evenlode.

STOW-ON-THE-WOLD

(15—SE) (4 miles South of Moreton-in-Marsh)
Focal point of the Northern Cotswolds, with eight
roads radiating from its windy site, seven hundred feet
above sea level. The best of Stow is centred upon its
large Market Square. Although none of the main roads
disurb it, the Square is alway busy with visitors in
summer time. There are several antique shops and
hotels overlooking the Square, but Stow has the happy

MAP 15   72

rt of catering for tourists without loosing dignity or charm. There is a medieval cross, although this has a headstone made in 1878.....the year that St. Edward's Hall was built (a little to the north). St. Edward's House overlooks them both, a handsome 18th century building with Corinthian pilasters.....all in mellow tone. The church lies between the square and the Fosse Way.....a large building dating back to the 12th century, much restored in the 17th century (having been used to house prisoners during the Civil War..... See Donnington, P 70), and restored again in the 19th century. Do not miss the impressive oil painting in the south aisle.

UPPER SLAUGHTER

(15—SW) (3 miles South West of Stow-on-the-Wold) The late Norman church was over-restored in 1877, but it has an attractively pinnacled tower, and a very grand monument to F.E. Witts, rector and lord of the manor, who died in 1854. The eight cottages by the church were re-modelled by Lutyens in 1906, and look agreeably trim, grouped around the small square.

The manor house is perhaps the finest example of Elizabethan architecture in the Cotswolds, but Upper Slaughter will always be remembered by the visitor for its road dropping down from the church to the ford, beneath a single massive tree. If you pass this way in mid afternoon, pause to watch the cattle being driven down the bank and across the stream bed towards the milking shed.....here is the very essence of the English countryside

UPPER SWELL

(15—SW) (1 mile North West of Stow-on-the-Wold) A small village, whose chief attraction lies in the bridge over the Dickler, where one can look up to the moss covered weir, and the mill pond beyond. The little church has a Norman doorway, and The Tudor Manor House beside it has a fine two storeyed porch, which is a splendid example of Cotswold domestic architecture.

Road to the church, Moreton-in-Marsh

At Upper Slaughter

The Weir, Upper Swell

The Mill, Upper Swell

Upper Slaughter Church

MAP 15

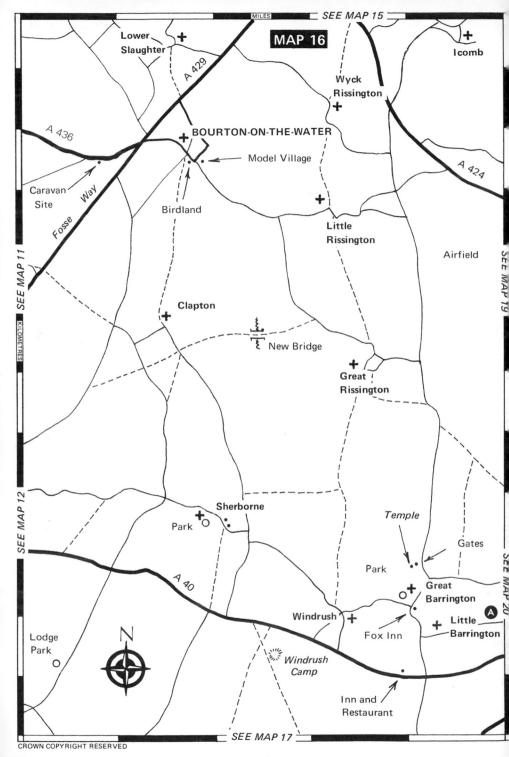

MILES

MAP 16

Lower Slaughter

Icomb

A 429

Wyck Rissington

BOURTON-ON-THE-WATER

A 436

Model Village

A 424

Caravan Site

Fosse Way

Birdland

Little Rissington

Airfield

KILOMETRES

Clapton

New Bridge

Great Rissington

Sherborne

Park

Temple

Gates

Park

A 40

Great Barrington

Windrush

Little Barrington

Fox Inn

Lodge Park

N

Windrush Camp

Inn and Restaurant

Map 16

The Middle Windrush and a Cotswold `Mecca'

BOURTON-ON-THE-WATER, THE BARRINGTONS, THE RISSINGTONS, LOWER SLAUGHTER, etc. . . .

BOURTON-ON-THE-WATER
(16—NW) (3 miles South West of Stow-on-the-Wold)
Here is the pre-eminent tourist mecca of the Cotswolds
—n unashamedly 'pretty' place, with a series of ornamental bridges spanning the clear waters of the Windrush, beside broad tree shaded greens. The church is an
odd mixture of styles, but the combination of 14th
century chancel, Georgian tower and Victorian nave,
has resulted in a pleasant, and certainly interesting
building. Apart from this there is a wealth of beautiful
buildings in Bourton-on-the-Water, but most visitors
will be more intent on visiting the Model Village, an
exact replica of the village in Cotswold stone, and
Birdland, a fascinating collection of exotic birds (also
penguins). There is also an excellent model railway
layout and in the old watermill, an interesting Motor
Museum.

Bourton-on-the-Water

It is now possible to walk around the newly
established 'Quarry Lakes'....flooded gravel workings,
in which wild fowl are becoming established. For
details, see the booklet 'Walks in the Cotswolds', which
caters excellently for walkers who wish to base them-
selves on Bourton-on-the-Water.

CLAPTON
(16—NW) (2 miles South of Bourton-on-the-Water)
An unpretentious little village on a hill looking across
the Windrush valley below Bourton-on-the-Water, to
the giant hangars of the old Rissington airfield on the
ridge beyond. Clapton has (not yet) been prettified, and
looks rather like a typical Cotswold village of the
early 1900's ....Claptonians, please do not arise in
anger.....this is intended as a compliment.

At the Model Village, Bourton-on-the-Water

The little church has simple late Norman features
(south doorway with plain tympanum and tub font),
although the pointed chancel arch is 'Early English'.
We liked the stone plaque proclaiming, *'Repairs
carried out 1951. The cost was heavy and was
cheerfully born, chiefly by the parishoners of Clapton
and Bourton-on-the-Water'.*

There is a pleasant 'bridle-road' across the Windrush
valley to Great Rissington, via New Bridge. This is
marked 'Unsuitable for Motor Vehicles', but we have
noticed local traffic still making use of it.

GREAT BARRINGTON
(16—SE) (3 miles West of Burford)
This is a small, quiet village with several pleasant 17th
and 18th century houses. It is dominated by Barrington
Park, a fine Palladian mansion built for Earl Talbot,
Lord Chancellor in the reign of George II, possibly by

Penguins at Birdland, Bourton-on-the-Water

At Great Rissington

William Kent. The house which overlooks a beautifull landscaped park through which the Windrush flows, not visible from the road, but the lovely wrought iro gates on the road from Great Rissington, and th exquisite classical temple visible through them, provid us with a tempting glimpse of 18th century splendour

The largely Norman church, which lies on the edg of the park, has an unusually high Norman chanc arch, and several interesting monuments, including delightfully sculptured memorial to Mary, Countes Talbot, by the fashionable 18th century sculpto Joseph Nollekens. Try to visit this church 'on the hour to hear the simple melody of its chiming clock.

GREAT RISSINGTON

(16—NE) (3 miles South East of Bourton-on-the-Water This village is spread out over the hillside, and it flower filled cottage gardens look out westward acros the wide Windrush valley. The main street runs dow hill from a little green towards the 17th century mano house. This together with the church make an attrac tive group, both showing clear evidence of sympatheti restoration and care. The cruciform church has a 15t century tower with pinnacles and battlements, and i the south transept there are three pleasing memoria tablets, especially that to John Barnard and his wife Do not miss the rather sad verse on the tablet t Thomas Cambray, nor the interesting little 15th cent ury carving of the crucifixion, re-set in the porch

The colourfully signed Lamb Inn is also a sma residential hotel, and should make a pleasant base fror which to explore this part of the Cotswolds.

Icomb

ICOMB

(16—NE) (2½ miles South East of Stow-on-the-Wold Attractive village tucked away beneath eight hundre foot high Icomb Hill, with almost every house and co tage a pleasure to the eye. The small church has blocked up Norman north doorway, and an 'Earl English' chancel, but it has all been rather heavily resto ed. Do not miss the effigy of Sir John Blaket (1431), knight in armour, and almost certainly the builder o Icomb Place, a fine medieval manor hidden away fror view at the south end of the village.

Windrush Valley near Little Barrington —
Map Ref. Ⓐ

LITTLE BARRINGTON

(16—SE) (3 miles West of Burforc An attractive village with houses surrounding a bow shaped green, which was originally a quarry. At leas two cottages have re-set medieval stone doorways. Th church has a Norman doorway and nave, but not especially, the charming memorial tablet built into th outer east wall of the porch. To the north east of th village there is a hospitable little inn called the Fo (Donnington Ales), overlooking an old bridge over th Windrush. About half a mile to the south, up on th busy A 40, there is an attractive hotel, with butter and restaurant.....a stone building now called the In for All Seasons.

There is a quiet road from Little Barrington t Burford, with mouth-watering views out over th Windrush.....real 'Wind in the Willows' country.

Spring at Little Rissington

MAP 16　　　　　76

ITTLE RISSINGTON

(16—NE) (1½ miles East of Bourton-on-the-Water)
mall village on the eastern slopes of the Windrush
alley, with views out over several flooded gravel pits
ee Bourton-on-the-Water, P 75). The church, which is
pproached by a footpath over the fields, has a Norman
uth doorway, but it was restored in the 19th century,
d is not of great interest.

ODGE PARK

(16—SW) (2½ miles South East of Northleach)
his charming little 17th century 'lodge' built by
ohn Dutton, a friend of Cromwell, in about 1650, was
signed as a 'grandstand' for those wishing to observe
er coursing in the surrounding park. It was only con-
erted into a dwelling in 1898, and is not open to the
blic. However a glimpse through the handsome 17th
ntury entrance gates will give a hint of its compact
d formal charms.

Lodge Park

OWER SLAUGHTER

(16—NW) (1½ miles North of Bourton-on-the-Water)
he whole village seems to have been planted upon the
anks of its stream, the two sides of which are linked
y a series of small bridges, all enchanting in their
mplicity. The water mill and its pond provide a fitting
trance for the stream and its departure is marked by
aceful willows, as it hurries away to join the River
ickler at Wyck Mill. Lower Slaughter is perhaps a
ttle over trim but it has wisely never been allowed to
mmercialise its charms. Even the attractive village
op is tucked away beside the bakehouse at the rear
f the mill, and is most modestly signed.

Lower Slaughter

HERBORNE

(16—SW) (4 miles South of Bourton-on-the-Water)
his village contains a charming row of cottages, set
nongst simple country gardens. The Post Office
arden is particularly attractive, and it would indeed be
ard to find a lovelier one anywhere. The church lies
ose to Sherborne Park and contains a beautiful
onument to Sir John Dutton by the celebrated 18th
entury sculptor, John Rysbrack, as well as several
ther interesting monuments to members of the
utton family.

Do not overlook the cottage with small re-set
orman arch, at the eastern end of the village.

INDRUSH

(16—SE) (4 miles West of Burford)
harming village above the Windrush meadows, with
leasant houses and cottages grouped around its small
riangular green. This is also overlooked by the hand-
ome Perpendicular tower of the church.....a pleasant
nd most interesting building. Its outstanding treasure
the beautiful Norman south doorway, with its
ouble row of grotesque beakheads, one of the best in
he Cotswolds. There is a lovely 15th century roof to
he nave, a medieval screen, a fine Jacobean pulpit, a
5th century font, some interesting medieval floor
les and a charming little sheep's head above the
rcading. In the churchyard there are a series of gorge-
us 18th century table tombs.

There is an Iron Age hill fort (Windrush Camp),
bout a mile to the south west, beside a bridle-way
ading over open country beyond the A 40.

South Doorway, Windrush

VYCK RISSINGTON see P 81.

MAP 16

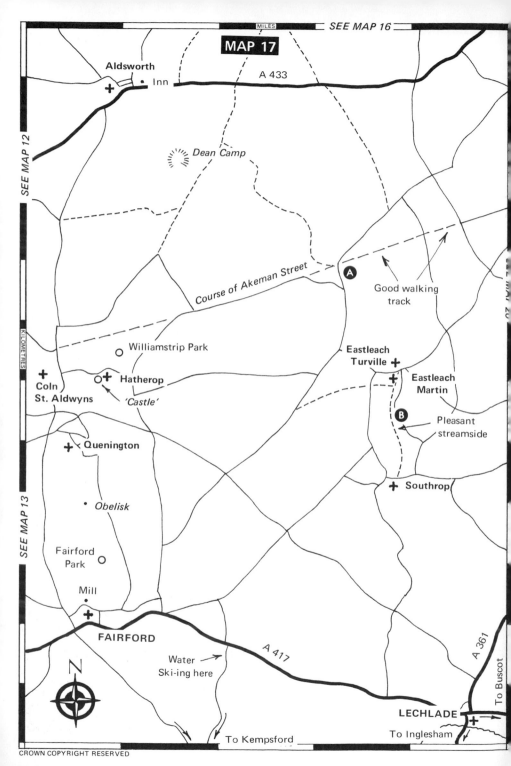

MILES

MAP 17

Aldsworth
• Inn

A 433

Dean Camp

Course of Akeman Street

Ⓐ

Good walking track

KILOMETRES

Williamstrip Park

Eastleach Turville

Eastleach Martin

Coln St. Aldwyns

Hatherop

'Castle'

Ⓑ

Pleasant streamside

Quenington

Southrop

Obelisk

Fairford Park

Mill
•

FAIRFORD

Water Ski-ing here

A 417

A 361

To Buscot

N

LECHLADE

To Inglesham

To Kempsford

78

Map 17

The Lower Leach and Coln Valleys

COLN ST. ALDWYNS, EASTLEACH, FAIRFORD, LECHLADE, etc. . . .

AKEMAN STREET

(On Maps 13—17—20 23—26)

Already dealt with on page 61, we only refer to it here in view of the exceptionally clear terrace remains of this road in the Leach valley (Map ref.  Ⓐ). This is visible from the road, although there is a bridle-way following the approximate course of the Akeman Street, in both directions from this point.

ALDSWORTH

(17—NW) (3 miles North East of Bibury)

The only building on the main A 433 is the Sherborne Arms, and mercifully the rest of the village is just far enough away to escape the traffic noise and fumes. Aldsworth's prosperity must have been at its peak when Bibury Racecourse was situated on the downs to its immediate south, and it still retains a solidly 18th and early 19th century flavour. The church and manor are a little distance to the west, beyond a rough green crossed by a stream almost engulfed in briars. The Norman church has a short dumpy spire, and sits comfortably in a rough sloping churchyard, with a fine collection of tomb stones for company. The perpendicular north aisle is a real beauty, being embellished with a splendid series of grotesque gargoyles outside, and with an elaborately carved niche within. Both porches are full of interest, but the north is particularly pleasing, with rib vaulting and a niche, thought to be for candles.....a possible 'poor man's chantry'. Do not miss this most interesting church.

'Akeman Street Valley' — Map Ref. Ⓐ

The Old Parsonage, Buscot

BUSCOT

(Off Map 17) (1½ miles South East of Lechlade on A 417)

It is possible to walk to Buscot along the Thames towpath from Lechlade, via St. John's Lock. Walk as far as Buscot Lock, and then cross the river and walk a short distance back along the willow bordered river, to the attractive church and the delicious 18th century 'Old Parsonage' close by. Buscot Park, a pleasant Adam style mansion (1780) set in a 55 acre park, lies to the south of the A 417, a mile beyond Buscot. It contains a fine collection of furniture and paintings, and is owned by the National Trust.

COLN ST. ALDWYNS

(17—NW) (2½ miles North of Fairford)

This is a lovely village, with a much restored church and an Elizabethan manor house looking out over the clear waters of the Coln, and the beech woods beyond. We found the interior of the church dull, but the

At Coln St. Aldwyns

MAP 17

Footbridge at Eastleach

War Memorial at Eastleach

Fairford Mill and Church

Hatherop Church

churchyard was bright with winter sunshine when we called, and crocus and snowdrops were growing amongst the beautifully sculptured tombstones below the trees. The yard of the New Inn was alive with the comings and goings of fan-tail doves, who seemed to sense the impending spring in the sun warmed air

EASTLEACH TURVILLE
and EASTLEACH MARTIN

(17–NE) (4 miles North of Lechlade)
The two parish churches solemnly regard each other across the little River Leach. Today Turville has the lion's share of the inhabitants, but Martin has the large church. Both churches are however very pleasant and unspoilt buildings (see the Norman tympanum to Turville south doorway, and the 14th century transept at Martin).

Take time off to wander up the slopes of Turville up past the war memorial, as far as the friendly little Victoria Inn, back down again, and across the little stone footbridge to Martin. If you pass this way in early spring you will be enchanted to find the banks of the Leach scattered with daffodils (but avoid weekend at this time if possible).

The road from Eastleach Martin to Southrop is open to the River Leach in places and provides one o two lovely places for picnicking (Map ref. **B**)

FAIRFORD

(17–SW) (4 miles West of Lechlade)
A warm little Cotswold town, with a broad street leading from the square to the magnificent 15th century church. This wonderfully proportioned building overlooking the Coln water-meadows was built by wool merchant, John Tame, and his son Edmund, in an age when Cotswold wool was renowned throughout Europe.

The Tames also gave the remarkably complete series of stained glass windows, which are Fairford' outstanding treasure. However do not overlook the fine oak beamed roof, with its attractive stone corbels the massive piers of the central tower, and the fascinating series of carved misericords beneath the choir stalls

Before you leave this most beautiful church, pause for a moment at John Tame's fine altar tomb, to remember the debt that we owe both to him and to the craftsmen he provided.

HATHEROP

(17–NW) (2½ miles North of Fairford)
This is largely a 19th century estate village, although several older houses have survived. Hatherop Castle is a 17th century manor house ambitiously enlarged and re-built complete with battlements in the 1850's. The 'French Gothic' church was the work of the same architect and contains a dramatic monument in white marble to Lady de Mauley.

INGLESHAM

(Off Map 17) (1 mile South of Lechlade on A 361)
We could not resist the inclusion of Inglesham church as it is a lovely little building by a farm beside the Thames, sensitively preserved by a man to whom we owe so much.....William Morris. Morris's work has left the medieval flavour of Inglesham undisturbed, and i is well worth visiting. Do not overlook the beautifully simple 13th century Madonna and Child.

MAP 17   80

LECHLADE

(17—SE) (4 miles East of Fairford)
Here on the southern borders of the Cotswolds, the
Coln and the Leach join the Thames, and in fact
Lechlade marks the head of its navigation. After 1789
it was possible to 'tranship' to narrow boats, for it was
from here that the Thames and Severn Canal (P 31)
started its long climb up over the Cotswolds. It was
also from here that stone was shipped down river for
St. Paul's and a multitude of other buildings in London
and Oxford (see Taynton Quarries, P 97).

The small market town of Lechlade is still busy
with the comings and going of boats, but now for
pleasure only. There are two fine bridges, Halfpenny
Bridge, by the boatyard, and St. John's Bridge beyond
meadows to the south east. The town is centred upon a
little market square, overlooked by dignified 18th and
early 19th century houses (see especially the mellow
brick, New Inn) and a fine Perpendicular ' 'wool
church', with its tower topped by a noble spire. The
interior is handsomely proportioned, with a high
clerestory and a magnificent chancel roof with carved
bosses. Do not miss the beautifully carved door leading
to the vestry, the 15th century brass of wool merchant,
John Townsend and his wife, nor the pleasant monument to Mrs. Simons (1769).

Boatyard at Lechlade

QUENINGTON

(17—SW) (2 miles North of Fairford)
Delicious village on the Coln, with pleasant houses and
cottages on its many slopes, notably Quenington
Court, with its circular dovecot and medieval gateway,
once the property of the Knights of St. John. The little
church has been over restored, but the Norman north
and south doorways, each with a richly carved
tympanum, should on no account be missed.

SOUTHROP

(17—SE) (2½ miles North of Lechlade)
Small village beside the willows and watermeadows of
the lovely River Leach, with a fine manor house and a
pleasant millhouse. There is a creeper clad inn called
the Swan, a pretty row of cottages, a gabled dovecot,
and tucked away beyond the manor, an interesting
little Norman church. John Keble, founder of the
'Oxford Movement' was curate here (1823—25) and he
was apparently responsible for re-discovering the
Norman font, which had been built into the south
doorway. This is a superb example of Norman craftsmanship, and in our view, the finest font in the
Cotswolds. Do not miss the 16th century effigies of
Sir John Conway and his lady.

Norman Doorway, Quenington

MAP 16 continued from P 77.

WYCK RISSINGTON

(16—NE) (1½ miles North East of
Bourton-on-the-Water)
Has a wide, rough green, about which are situated
many attractive houses and cottages, the most pleasing
of which is a farmhouse fronting on to a well stocked
duck pond. The church has a massive, squat Norman
tower and a beautifully tended churchyard where
amongst the roses, will be found the grave of 'James
Loveridge, Gipsy'. On his tombstone is proudly
proclaimed.....'Of No Fixed Abode'.....a tribute to a
traveller whose final journey ended at Wyck Rissington.

Norman Font, Southrop

MAP 17

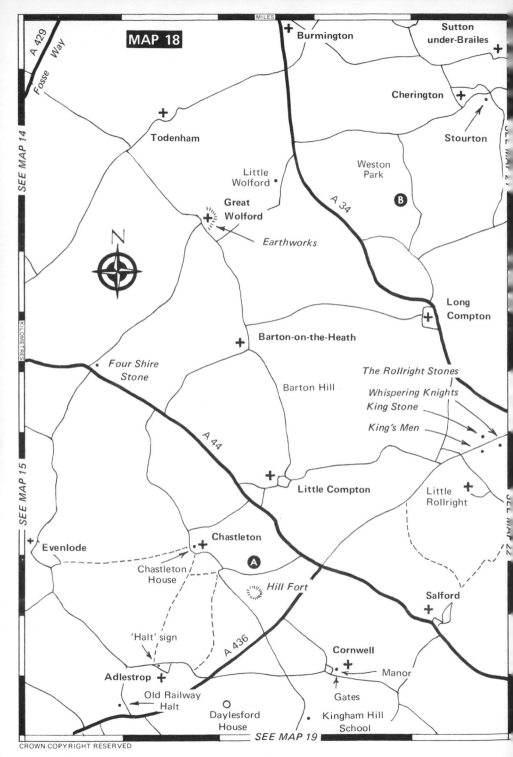

MAP 18

MILES

A 429

Fosse Way

SEE MAP 14

KILOMETRES

SEE MAP 15

Burmington

Sutton under-Brailes

Cherington

Stourton

Todenham

Little Wolford

Weston Park

B

A 34

Great Wolford

Earthworks

Long Compton

N

Four Shire Stone

Barton-on-the-Heath

Barton Hill

The Rollright Stones

Whispering Knights

King Stone

King's Men

A 44

Little Compton

Little Rollright

SEE MAP 22

Evenlode

Chastleton

A

Salford

Chastleton House

Hill Fort

'Halt' sign

A 436

Cornwell

Manor

Adlestrop

Old Railway Halt

Gates

Daylesford House

Kingham Hill School

SEE MAP 19

Map 18

Four Shires Country

CHASTLETON HOUSE, CORNWELL, LONG COMPTON, ROLLRIGHT STONES, etc. . . .

ADLESTROP

(18—SW) (3 miles East of Stow-on-the-Wold) Quiet village with pleasant houses in a cul-de-sac by the church. Adlestrop House was once the rectory, and Jane Austen used to stay here with her uncle, Theophilus Leigh. Adlestrop Park was re-built in the Gothick style by Sanderson Miller (see Edge Hill, P 100), in 1762, and the grounds were laid out by Humphrey Repton. The church stands in an immaculate churchyard, but we found the interior too 'tidy' for our taste.

Adlestrop will always be remembered as the subject of Edward Thomas's poem 'Adlestrop' the first two verses of which run:

'Adlestrop.....only a name'

> *Yes, I remember Adlestrop.....*
> *The name.....because one afternoon*
> *Of heat the express-train drew up there*
> *Unwontedly. It was late June.*
>
> *The steam hissed. Someone cleared his throat,*
> *No one left and no one came*
> *On the bare platform. What I saw*
> *Was Adlestrop.....only a name.*

The station has been closed, but the sign and the station bench now stand in a small shelter in Adlestrop.....a tribute to Thomas by the village he immortalised.

BARTON-ON-THE-HEATH

(18— NW) (3 miles East of Moreton-in-Marsh) Is centred upon an attractive green with an unusual domed 'well head' memorial amongst the trees. This is overlooked by 17th century Barton House, beyond which lies the Norman church, with its small saddleback tower. Two sculptural details provide a clue to the presence of an earlier Anglo-Danish building (unusual so far to the south west) and there is also an amusing fragment of Norman sculpture.....of a pig running up the chancel arch. Do not overlook the small brass to Edmund Bury (1559).

The Green, Barton-on-the-Heath

Captain Robert Dover, 17th century lawyer, and founder of the Cotswold Games (P 49), lived here for some years.

BURMINGTON

(18—NE) (5 miles North East of Moreton-in-Marsh) An unassuming village above the Stour valley with a modest, largely Victorian church in a well mown churchyard, backed by the manor house. The only items of interest inside are the Norman corbels, which

Barn At Burmington

Chastleton House

Dovecot, Chastleton

Open Road above Chastleton — Map Ref.

Spring Sunshine, Cornwell

have been incorporated into the chancel arch.

The attractive little Victorian school is now converted into a village hall, and there is a fascinating brick and timber barn on saddle stones, a short distance away.....its materials reminding us that we are straying too far from Cotswold stone country.

We talked in Burmington churchyard to an old man who told us that he was born in one of the cottages opposite the church, and that he hopes to die there too. How humbling to encounter such contentment and stability in our restless and ever changing world.

CHASTLETON

(18—SW) (3 miles South East of Moreton-in-Marsh) Small village on the lower slopes of the Cotswolds dominated by Chastleton House, a dignified Stuart manor house, built by Walter Jones, a wool merchant from Witney. The house, which was sadly in need of attention when we last called, remains unspoilt by 18th or 19th century alteration, and it is to this good fortune that we owe the perfect Long Gallery, with beautifully plastered ceiling. There is a topiary garden to the side of the house, an attractive arched dovecot across the road, and medieval barns close by. The adjoining church has some colourful medieval floor tiles and two interesting brasses (1592) (1631) depicting styles of dress at the turn of the century.

On Chastleton Hill there is a pleasant stretch of open road (Map ref. Ⓐ). running across to the A 44 with fine views out over the Evenlode valley. A little further to the south is Chastleton Burrow, a well preserved, circular Iron Age hill fort, whose banks are now thickly wooded. These banks were faced with large blocks of stone (some of which survive).....an unusual feature in an Iron Age fortification.

CHERINGTON

(18—NE) (6 miles North East of Moreton-in-Marsh) Comfortably situated in the upper Stour valley between Brailes Hill and Stourton Hill, Cherington is a model stone village, with a handsome late 17th century manor house and a church that is full of interest. Rose trees line the path to the south porch of this largely 13th century building. It has a well proportioned tower, some fine Perpendicular windows, some with interesting medieval glass, a Jacobean altar table and rail, and a delightful series of carved corbel figures beneath the roof beams. However Cherington's greatest treasure is the lovely 14th century canopied tomb chest, topped with an effigy of a 'civilian', whose name is not known, a fine specimen of the 'Decorated' period.

CORNWELL

(18—SE) (3 miles West of Chipping Norton) A delicious little village, lovingly restored by Clough Williams-Ellis, who has added a touch of his own Portmeirion's flavour in the shape of the little bow fronted shop. A short distance along the road toward Chipping Norton, there is a glimpse of the enchanting manor house through wrought iron gates to the left. The small church lies in parkland beyond the village (walk behind manor), and has a pleasant although heavily restored interior. Do not overlook the font with its base of four lions.

DAYLESFORD HOUSE

(18—SW) (See Daylesford, P89—90)

MAP 18   84

EVENLODE

(18—SW) (2 miles South East of Moreton-in-Marsh) idespread village in the broad upper Evenlode valley, ith a Georgian rectory and several pleasant farm- ouses, one with pretty Gothick windows. The old hool used to house an attractive collection of toys, it sadly this has now departed. The church lies on the estern edge of the village in a churchyard containing veral interesting 18th and 19th century tombs. It has fine late Norman chancel arch, with a mason's mark the south side, a pretty rood loft stair and a carved 5th century oak pulpit. All the items of interest are belled with little cards, which we consider to be an cellent idea.

Farmhouse at Evenlode

OUR SHIRE STONE

(18—NW) (1½ miles East of Moreton-in-Marsh) handsome 18th century monument topped by a ndial and ball, marking the meeting of the four ounties of Oxfordshire, Gloucestershire, Warwick- ire and Worcestershire (although the isolated 'island' Worcestershire has been swallowed up in Gloucester- ire long ago). This monument stands at a cross roads the A 44, and is unfortunately overshadowed by ees and a bushy hedge.

REAT WOLFORD

(18—NW) (3 miles North East of Moreton-in-Marsh) n unpretentious village close to the watershed tween the Stour (north to the Avon) and the Even- de (south to the Thames). Although it stands less than ur hundred feet above sea level, it has the remains f an Iron Age hill fort to its south and east. The urch was re-built in the 19th century, but its tall ire is a most impressive landmark.

Four Shire Stone   *Monument at Little Rollright*

ITTLE COMPTON

(18—SE) (4 miles South East of Moreton-in-Marsh) ying in a pleasant hollow between Barton Hill and the ain Cotswold edge. Little Compton is Warwickshire's uthern-most village. The lovely 17th century manor ouse was the home of Archbishop Juxon, who attend- d Charles I at his trial and subsequent execution on e scaffold outside Whitehall. Hidden away in the ounds is a gabled dovecot. The church next door tains its 14th century tower with saddle-back roof, ut the remainder was re-built in the 19th century and not of great interest to visitors.

Little Compton Manor

ITTLE ROLLRIGHT CHURCH

(18—SE) (2 miles North West of Chipping Norton) his lies beyond a fine manor house and a few cottages a quiet setting beneath the hills. It has a simple terior, full of atmosphere, with pleasant Perpendicu- r windows and two gorgeous 17th century monu ents, which should on no account be missed.

ITTLE WOLFORD

(18—NE) (4 miles North East of Moreton-in-Marsh) his would be a totally unexciting hamlet were it not or the presence of its delicious 16th century manor ouse, tantalising glimpses of which are obtainable om the road. We particularly delight in its mixture f stone and timber-framing.....appropriate in an area ving between the Cotswold hills and the forest lands f Warwickshire.

Little Rollright Church

MAP 18

LONG COMPTON

(18—NE) (4 miles North West of Chipping Norton)
Poor Long Compton still remains a hostage to th
over busy A 34 and waits patiently for some form o
relief. It stretches out along this main road for ove
half a mile, to the very foot of the long hill, climbin
the Cotswold edge. It has a cheerful inn, many trin
houses and cottages, and a church whose handsom
Perpendicular tower looks westwards out over a larg
bumpy field which we suspect to be the site of th
original village. The lovely south porch is reached by
yew lined path, which is approached beneath a delight
ful little two storeyed lych gate, believed to be a smal
timber-framed cottage, with its lower storey removed
The core of the church is 13th century, but externall
it appears to be almost entirely Perpendicular. See th
nave roof, the charming little Perpendicular south aisl
chapel and the pathetically worn effigy of a lady in th
porch (this one really does appear to have been use
for the sharpening of scythes, and when we called her
last, there were in fact two scythes hanging immediate
ly above it..... We are sure this is now only coincidental)

Long Compton

The King's Men, Rollright

ROLLRIGHT STONES

(18—SE) (2½ miles North West of Chipping Norton)
These consist of three separate features:

1. **The King's Men** A Bronze Age stone circle, about
   hundred feet in diameter (about 2000—1800 BC)
   lying to the immediate south of a road between th
   A 34 and A 44.

2. **The Whispering Knights** The remains of a Bronz
   Age burial chamber, 400 yards to the east of th
   circle.

3. **The King Stone** An isolated 'standing stone', nearl
   opposite the King's Men, and almost certainly asso
   ciated with them, although its exact purpose is no
   known.

These all lie in fine upland country, and there ar
splendid views, especially northwards from the Kin
Stone, but all these monuments have suffered th
indignity of enclosure (no doubt of necessity, thanks t
idiot vandalism).

The Rollright Stones are the subject of a medieva
legend of a king intent on the conquest of England
who was confronted by a witch who spoke as follows:

The Whispering Knights, Rollright

> *'If Long Compton thou canst see,*
> *King of England thou shalt be.'*

Unfortunately for the king and his followers thi
proved to be impossible, and the witch continued....

> *'As Long Compton thou canst not see*
> *King of England thou shalt not be.*
> *Rise up stick, and stand still, stone,*
> *For King of England thou shalt be none.*
> *Thou and thy men hoar stones shalt be,*
> *And I shall be an eldern tree.'*

At this stage, the King, his men and his knights were al
turned into stone and the witch became an elder tree..
a sorry tale, but it must have been good material for th
peasants of Long Compton during those long medieva
winter evenings.

The King Stone, Rollright   *Long Compton Church*

MAP 18   86

SALFORD

(18—SE) (2 miles West of Chipping Norton)
A small village mercifully just off the A 34, with no special features of interest apart from its church, which was largely re-built by our favourite Victorian architect, G.E. Street...although this is not one of his better jobs. However there is the base of an old cross in the churchyard, an interesting Norman font with interlaced arcading, and a crudely carved Sagittarius the Archer on a tympanum over the north doorway. This subject was quite a favourite in the Cotswold area.....see also Kencot (P 96) and Hook Norton (P 105).

Salford Church

STOURTON

(18—NE) (6½ miles North East of Moreton-in-Marsh)
This is virtually a continuation of Cherington (P 84), but it lies closer to the Stour than its neighbour. There are several pleasant old houses, including two mills on the Stour.

TODENHAM

(18—NW) (3 miles North East of Moreton-in-Marsh)
A pleasantly unspoilt village with a dignified late Georgian manor house, and little 18th century mellow brick inn, the Farrier's Arms, which has so far escaped the notice of the brewery restorers and which therefore still has a real rural flavour. The largely 14th century church has a fine tower and spire. The little priest's door on the south side is a charming example of the Decorated' style, but on the north side will be found Perpendicular windows added by the Grevilles in the course of building a north chapel and north aisle in the 16th century. Do not overlook the 13th century font, the brass to William Molton (1614), nor the macabre memorial tablet on the outside south wall.

Memorial Tablet, Todenham   *Priest's Door, Todenham*

WESTON PARK

(18—NE) (5 miles North East of Moreton-in-Marsh)
A delightful area of parkland bereft of its mansion, which was apparently pulled down in the 1920's, but must have been early 19th century in style, if the surviving lodges are any indication. However we include it here, as there is an open public road through the park (Map ref. **B**) between Cherington and Long Compton, which makes an extremely pleasant walk. Please do not trespass away from the road.

In Weston Park — Map Ref. **B**

MAP 11 continued from P 55.

TEMPLE GUITING

(11—NW) (4 miles East of Winchcombe)
A deep, secret place, with pools both above and below the small bridge over the infant Windrush. There is a small bow-fronted shop, and several pleasant houses including elegant 18th century Guiting House, which looks across the small wooded valley to the church. This was once owned by the Knights Templar, but only fragments of their Norman church remain. The architectural history of the church is very involved, and restoration and rebuilding has taken place several times. However we liked the 18th and 19th century tower and the exceptionally handsome Royal Arms of George III in white plaster.

Temple Guiting Church (See Map 11)

MAP 18

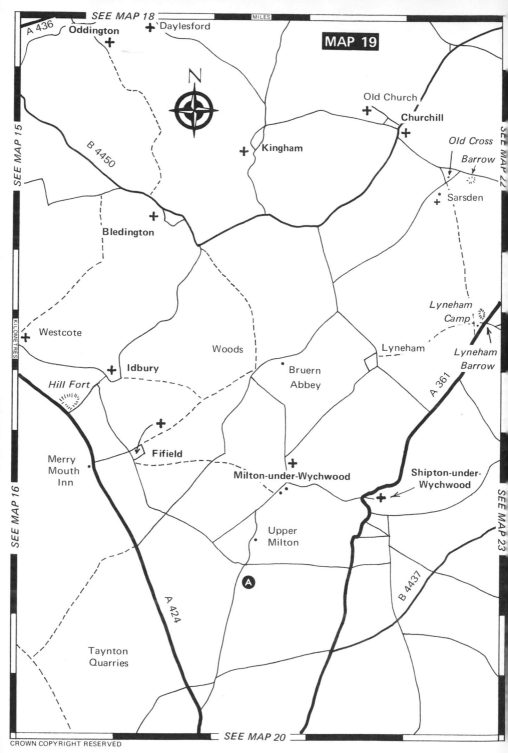

SEE MAP 18

A 436
Oddington
Daylesford

MILES

MAP 19

N

Old Church
Churchill

SEE MAP 15

B 4450

Kingham

Old Cross
Barrow

Sarsden

Bledington

SEE MAP 22

Westcote

Woods

Lyneham
Camp

SEE MAP 16

KILOMETRES

Idbury

Hill Fort

Fifield

Merry
Mouth
Inn

Bruern
Abbey

Lyneham

Lyneham
Barrow

A 361

Milton-under-Wychwood

Upper
Milton

A

Taynton
Quarries

A 424

Shipton-under-
Wychwood

B 4437

SEE MAP 23

SEE MAP 20

Map 19

The Broad Evenlode Valley

CHURCHILL, DAYLESFORD, KINGHAM, SHIPTON-UNDER-WYCHWOOD, etc. . . .

BLEDINGTON

(19—NW) (4 miles South East of Stow-on-the-Wold)
Sprawling village in the Evenlode valley with some
modern development. However there is a wide green,
complete with small inn, the King's Arms, and a stream
with noisy ducks. Moreover before we reach this we
come upon the church, sitting quietly on the southern
fringe of the village, with a row of attractive cottages
overlooking its churchyard. Although it has earlier
origins, most of the good things in this church are from
the 15th century, with fine roofs to nave and chancel,
lovely old doorway with its original door, and above all,
the splendid series of Perpendicular windows, several
of which contain really beautiful stained glass. This is
believed to be the work of John Prudde, the Westminster craftman who produced the glass in Warwick's
Beauchamp Chapel. The money for all these improve-
ments came from prosperous Winchcombe Abbey, who
held the living here.

Bledington Church

BRUERN ABBEY

(19—NE) (5 miles North of Burford)
A Cistercian abbey was founded here in the reign of
King Stephen, but the dignified 18th century mansion
glimpsed from the road lies a little to the north of its
original site, beside the banks of the Evenlode. The
abbey was sold to Sir Thomas Brydges soon after the
dissolution (1539) and the last abbot ended his days as
rector of Wigginton (P 122).
There is very little to see at Bruern, but the roads
leading to it from south and east pass pleasant woodlands, and there is a charming mill house on the Evenlode, close to the mansion.

Evenlode Valley Country — Map Ref. Ⓐ

CHURCHILL

(19—NE) (2½ miles South West of Chipping Norton)
The early 19th century church was re-modelled on various Oxford buildings, the tower being a one third
replica of Magdalen's The somewhat bizarre 'fountain'
should interest lovers of Victorian gothic, but appears
to be out of context here. Only the chancel of the old
church remains, sited beyond an old arch, looking
across the Evenlode valley towards Daylesford Park.
Warren Hastings (see Daylesford below) was born in a
house which lies on the road between the two churches.

DAYLESFORD

(19—NW) (4 miles East of Stow-on-the-Wold)
Daylesford House is not visible from any road, but it is
a fine mansion, built in Hornton stone by S.P. Cocker-

Churchill Church

89

MAP 19

ell, the architect of Sezincote, for the great Warren Hastings on his return from his controversial career i India. There is a miniature estate village at the gates and a splendidly elaborate Victorian church by J.L Pearson, the architect of Truro Cathedral. See especially Pearson's pretty tub shaped pulpit, the brass t William Gardiner (1632) and the elegant monumen outside the east window, simply inscribed 'Warren Hastings 1818'.

FIFIELD

(19—SW) (4 miles North of Burford)
A modest village looking out over the Evenlode valle towards Bruern Woods, the source of timber for th hurdle makers that worked here for centuries (this craf survived at Fifield until the 1950's). The church stand in a wide, open churchyard and has a minute 14t century spire. Although much restored, it is wort visiting, if only to look at the charming 17th centur brass of Mary Palmer, complete with eight childre and a baby in christening robes. The hospitable Merr Mouth Inn (Donnington Ales) on the high A 424 derives its unusual title from a local family th Merrimonts.

IDBURY

(19—NW) (4½ miles South East of Stow-on-the-Wold
Situated on eastern slopes beneath the high wolds where there are the earthworks of an Iron Age hill for close to the A 424, Idbury is a minute village lookin out over the Evenlode valley, with a pleasant bridle way down to Bruern Woods. The lovely Tudor manor house was once the editorial headquarters of tha delightful little magazine, the Countryman* (the foun ding editor, Robertson Scott lived here) and there is a tablet over the door inscribed *'Oh more than happy countrymen, if he but knew his good fortune'.* There is also a poignant tablet in a wall by the roadside inscribed *'This tree is planted in proud memory o Peter Scott, A.F.C. of Idbury, who died in 1943, ir Canada'.*

The largely Perpendicular church has a blocked up Norman doorway, a beautiful 15th century nave roo supported on corbel figures, a pulpit made up from three medieval bench ends, bench ends of the same period, and a particularly lovely octagonal font. Bu more important than these separate details, is the unspoilt medieval atmosphere that lingers here. In the churchyard will be found the tomb of Sir Benjamir Baker, the civil engineer that designed the origina Assuan Dam and the famous Forth Railway Bridge

*Editorial offices of the Countryman have been a Burford for many years.

KINGHAM

(19—NW) (4 miles South West of Chipping Norton)
Large village in the broad Evenlode valley with wide open greens at its northern end and a very handsome 17th century rectory near the southern end. Beyond the rectory, the small tower of Kingham church looks out across the Evenlode meadows. When we last called the interior was being re-painted, but we could see the unusual stone pew ends and backs.....all part of the restoration of 1853, and very cold in appearance. Do not overlook the brass of Katherine James (1588).

Font at Idbury

The Green, Kingham

The Old Rectory, Kingham

LYNEHAM

(19—NE) (5 miles North of Burford)

Small village in flat Evenlode country, with an early 19th century flavour further enhanced by its Methodist chapel. It is not an unduly interesting village, but on high ground away to the east (to the immediate west of the A 361) there are the remains of a long barrow, with a single stone standing at its north east end, and an Iron Age hill fort a short distance beyond to the north east.

MILTON-UNDER-WYCHWOOD

(19—SE) (4 miles North of Burford)

The church, in this widespread village in the Evenlode valley, was designed by G.E. Street, best known for the Law Courts in the Strand, and our favourite Victorian architect. Church, lych-gate, vicarage and school.....all stand witness to his ability. The village street beyond the Quart Pot, has a pleasant series of shops and houses, but apart from the stone bull's head above the butcher's shop, there is nothing of exceptional interest.

Curiosity Shop, Milton-under-Wychwood

ODDINGTON

(19—NW) (2½ miles East of Stow-on-the-Wold)

An attractive village spread-eagled on the lower slopes of the hill between Stow and the Evenlode. It has several interesting old houses, two inns, the Fox and the Horse and Groom, and an unassuming Victorian new' church.

Oddington's old church lies by itself at the end of a road south of the village, although there is a long bridle-way onwards from here to Bledington. There were primroses in its pretty churchyard when we last called, and we were delighted by the wonderfully unspoilt interior. See especially the Jacobean pulpit on its turned newel post, the beautiful old chancel roof, the 15th century font, and Oddington's great treasure... its extensive (and horrific) 'Doom' wall painting. No wonder the medieval clergy were able to keep the peasants 'God fearing'.

Wall Painting, Oddington

SARSDEN

(19—NE) (3 miles South West of Chipping Norton)

A quiet hamlet in rolling wooded parkland, with two round barrows, a medieval wayside cross, and a beautiful 18th century mansion. This has a church of the same period right beside it.....an austere building with little of interest for the visitor.

SHIPTON-UNDER-WYCHWOOD

(19—SE) (4 miles North East of Burford)

Large village on the River Evenlode, with several very pleasant old houses, a fine wide green between the lovely old Shaven Crown Hotel (once a hospice run by the monks of Bruern, P 89) and the tall spired church. This has a 15th century vaulted porch and a large, rather bleak interior. It does however contain a handsome 15th century stone pulpit, a large font of the same period, and a charming Tudor wall monument with husband and wife at a prayer desk, accompanied by their children.

Font at Oddington   *The Shaven Crown, Shipton-under-Wychwood*

TAYNTON STONE QUARRIES

(19—SW) (See Taynton, P 97)

WESTCOTE see P 97.

Shipton-under-Wychwood

MAP 19

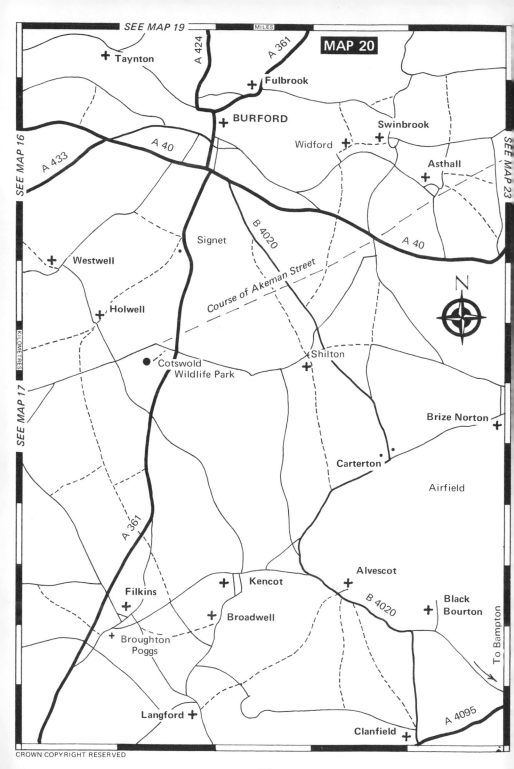

Map 20

Windrush Country and a Wildlife Park

BURFORD, LANGFORD, SHILTON, SWINBROOK, TAYNTON, etc. . . .

ALVESCOT

(20- SE) (5 miles North East of Lechlade)
Sits comfortably astride the busy B 4020, and seems determined not to be disturbed either by this, or the noisy aircraft from the great runways of Brize Norton just to the north. There are two inns.....the Plough, which lies rather inappropriately opposite a quaint little Strict Baptist chapel, and the Red Lion, a little further down the street. There is a small road between the two pubs, leading to the church, which lies in a quiet setting to the north of the village. This is a pleasant cruciform building, with a well proportioned Perpendicular tower, and a good 14th century south doorway. Inside, there are lovely old roof timbers resting on carved corbels, some handsome 18th century wall monuments, and brasses in the south aisle of Alice Malory (1579), complete with husband and children.

Alvescot Church

ASTHALL

(20—NE) (2½ miles East of Burford)
This is one of the classic Windrush villages, complete with water meadows willow trees, gabled Elizabethan manor overlooking small church, and a tidy little inn. No single item is exceptional, but together they spell perfection.

Victorian restoration has not been too kind to the interior of the church, but the medieval glass in the north chapel windows and the 14th century effigy of a lady with wimple and flowing robes are well worth looking at. Also do not overlook the charming 18th century table tomb in the churchyard.

BAMPTON

(To South East of Map 20)
(4½ miles South West of Witney)
Once known as Bampton in the Bush, it is a quiet market town which has the good fortune to be 'miles from anywhere'. It has many pleasant 17th and 18th century houses, a few inns and a minute Town Hall, but its only building of outstanding interest is the church. This has a splendid 170 feet high spire, at whose base are four flying buttresses, each surmounted by a carved apostle. The contents of the interior include canopied sedilia in the chancel, a fine stone reredos, three brasses and an impressive 17th century monument (George Thomas, 1603).

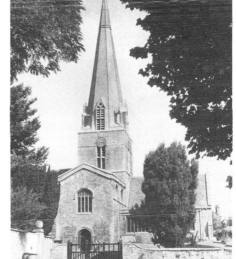

Bampton Church

MAP 20

Tympanum at Black Bourton

Wall Painting, Black Bourton

View from Broadwell Porch

South Doorway, Brize Norton

Burford Bridge

BLACK BOURTON

(20—SE) (5 miles South West of Witney
Small village on a road cut off by the builders of Brize
Norton airfield.....at least there is less traffic noise
which compensates a little for the monstrous howl o
great jet aircraft, to which this village is subjected
There are bungalows and Victorian estate houses, bu
the church, which lies just south of the gaily signee
Horse and Groom, is well worth visiting.

There is a pretty little Norman priest's doorway
and a large porch leading into a pleasingly plasterec
interior, which is full of a flavour of the past. The out
standing treasure here is the series of splendid 13th
century wall paintings, but do not overlook the attrac
tive stone corbel figures, and the monument to Lad
Hungerford (1592), all in pale stone.

BRIZE NORTON

(20—SE) (3 miles West of Witney
Here is a once quiet village on the Cotswold fringes
well nigh drowned by the noise and activity generatec
by the great airfield on its doorstep. However the
church still stands in its neat churchyard, enriched by
lovely old table tombs, and there is a satisfactory Nor
man south doorway within its medieval porch. Do no
overlook the Norman font with its arcade decoration
nor the 14th century effigy of a knight.

BROADWELL

(20—SW) (3½ miles North East of Lechlade
Small village not far to the north of flat Thames grave
country, with two stone gate pillars, the only surviving
evidence of a long vanished manor house. There are
however several pleasant stone houses and a character
inn, called the Five Bells.

The cruciform church has a fine 13th century stone
spire, which appears to have a slight twist, and by the
churchyard gate, the extensive remains of a medieva
cross. The Norman south doorway has unfortunately
been so heavily restored that it has lost its true
character; and this is also true of the interior of the
church. There is a tall Norman tower arch, but the
walls have been ruthlessly scraped, and there are shiny
tiles and pitch-pine pews much in evidence. However
do not overlook the dramatic Victorian glass depicting
the Three Kings, nor the wall monuments to John
Huband (1668) and Sophia Colston (1802).

BROUGHTON POGGS

(20—SW) (See Filkins, P 95.

BURFORD

(20—NW) (9 miles South East of Stow-on-the-Wold
Has an impressively wide main street dropping down
from the wolds to the Windrush valley. The river is
crossed by a fine medieval bridge, which has so far
resisted the pressures of the highway improvers. The
dignified church has a Norman tower capped with a
slender 15th century spire. See the tombs of Sir Lawr
ence Tanfield, and Speaker Lenthall, the Member of
Parliament who defied Charles I.

See also the Almshouses, the Grammar School, the
little Tolsey Museum, and the 'Palladian' Methodist
Chapel. However if you really wish to appreciate
Burford, take time to walk the whole length of the
High Street, and also take the quiet footpath westwards
from the bridge along the banks of the Windrush.

MAP 20　　　　　94

CARTERTON

(20—SE) (4 miles South East of Burford)
This can best be described as a 'garrison town' for Brize Norton airfield and is very different in character to the surrounding countryside. It does however have heated open-air swimming pools set in a beautiful recreation ground, and for this reason is worth visiting.

CLANFIELD

(20—SE) (4 miles North of Faringdon)
Long straggling village less than two miles north of the Thames but still predominantly Cotswold in flavour. It has two attractive inns, the Plough and the Mason's Arms.

The interior of the church is cold from over-restoration, but the exterior is well proportioned and is enlivened by a carving of St. Stephen high up on the 14th century tower, complete with the symbols of his martyrdom.....four stones.

High Street, Burford

COTSWOLD WILDLIFE PARK, BRADWELL GROVE

(20—NW) (3 miles South of Burford)
A splendid wildlife collection in the wooded grounds of Bradwell Grove, an early 19th century mansion in the Gothic style. It is attractively laid out, and contains an interesting collection of animals and birds including llamas, flamingoes, penguins, leopards, red pandas, and white rhino. Many of the smaller animals are displayed in the old walled garden, while others virtually roam free in woodlands and paddock enclosures. There are pony and donkey rides and an adventure playground; and the booklet describing the Park is the best zoo publication that we have yet encountered.

Clanfield Church

FILKINS and BROUGHTON POGGS

(20—SW) (3½ miles North East of Lechlade)
This is now virtually one long village, and all is happily by-passed by the busy A 361. Broughton Poggs church is a small Norman building with a squat saddle-back tower. tucked away behind farm buildings (access via drive-way to Broughton Hall and not via farmyard). It has two small Norman doorways and a narrow Norman chancel arch.

Not far to the north is the cheerful Five Alls, an inn with a restaurant, and then beyond it is Filkins church. This was designed by G.E. Street (see Milton-under-Wychwood, P 91) and is a pleasant 19th century building. We must admit however that our favourite building in Filkins is the Lamb Inn, splendidly clad in Virginia creeper. A small but interesting museum containing local byegones was established here many years ago by Sir Stafford and Lady Cripps.....ask locally for further details.

The Post Office, Filkins

FULBROOK

(20—NW) (¾ mile North East of Burford)
Large village astride the A 361, and only separated from Burford by the Windrush and its watermeadows, It has an interesting church just away from the main road. This has a beautiful Norman south doorway, a fine 16th century roof supported on well carved corbel figures, a series of solid 12th century arcade capitals and an opulently colourful 17th century monument in the chancel. The Carpenter's Arms looks pleasant, although we must admit that we have our favourites across the Windrush in nearby Burford, and have not therefore sampled it.

South Porch, Fulbrook

MAP 20

War Memorial, Holwell

South Porch, Kencot

Saxon Crucifix, Langford

Village Pond, Shilton

HOLWELL

(20—NW) (2½ miles South West of Burford
Quiet hamlet in wold country with pleasant farr
buildings not far from the small modern church (1910
Do not overlook the beautifully carved wooden panel
(German or Flemish?) incorporated in the pulpit

KENCOT

(20—SW) (4 miles North East of Lechlade
This attractive village to the immediate north o
Broadwell (P 94) has the misfortune to lie close t
Brize Norton airfield and from time to time durin
our brief visit, the air around us seemed to be rippe
apart by noise. However flying does not go on *all* th
time, and Kencot is an otherwise quiet village, with
cabinet making workshop at its southern end (see th
attractive squirrel sign), and an interesting little churc
beyond a minute triangular green. It has an unusua
turret stair and a Norman south doorway with
tympanum depicting Sagittarius the Archer (quite
favourite in this area.....see Salford, P 87 and Hoo
Norton, P105). The interior of the church has bee
restored as recently as 1962((*'This made possible b*
the generousity of Edith Bundy of San Francisco',
modest notice proclaims).....Thank you Mrs. Bundy
There is a pleasant little early 19th century gallery,
Jacobean pulpit and a 17th century monument t
Mary Oldisworth and Elizabeth Mountsteven.

LANGFORD

(20—SW) (3 miles North East of Lechlade
A quiet village looking south towards flat Thame
valley farmland, and the distant Berkshire Down
beyond. Langford's church is a little treasure house o
medieval art and architecture and should not be missec
Built into the south porch, is a rare and beautiful Saxo
carving of the Crucifixion and a 14th century carvin
with the figures of Mary and John. There are als
other fascinating figures carved on the Norman tower
The Norman and Early English arches beneath th
tower of this cruciform church are unusually lofty an
on a sunny day one could imagine oneself to be i
Provence rather than in Oxfordshire.

SHILTON

(20—NE) (2½ miles South East of Burford
A very lovely village tucked away in the quiet valle
of the Shill Brook, just below the busy B 4020, an
only a mile from the 'garrison town' of Cartertor
Shilton has everything.....a stream, a pond edged wit
chestnut trees and a ford with a road leading u
beside a farm and dovecote. It has rose decked cottages
flower filled gardens and a small but very friendly in
(the Rose and Crown) where we once had deliciou
ham rolls and draught Guiness sitting in the warr
sunshine. Church and rectory lie to the south of th
village, and in the church we found an exceptionall
beautiful Norman font, enriched with later (14t
century) carving. We found Shilton so enchanting tha
we quite forgot out earlier visit to Carterton, and th
occasional sound of aircraft seemed somehow mor
remote.

SWINBROOK

(20—NE) (2 miles East of Burford
A delectable village, whose rough sloping green i
enlivened by a small stream, and whose church must o
no account be passed by. A fine Perpendicular window

MAP 20   96

lls the whole of its east end and light floods in upon two
orgeous 'three-decker' wall tombs, in which there are six
nale members of the Fettiplace family, all lying on their right
des, looking not upwards but outwards. See also the carved
nedieval chancel stalls.

In the churchyard there are the gravestones of Unity
Mitford and her sister Nancy, whose childhood years in
winbrook are so wonderfully described by their sister Jessica
n Hons and Rebels.

Spring at Swinbrook

AYNTON

(20—NW) (1½ miles North West of Burford)
rim stone village in the Windrush valley, with views
ut towards the willow bordered river that always
eminds an American friend of ours of Ratty and
Iole's 'Wind in the Willows'. Yew trees line the wide
ath to the north door of the church, overlooked by
aynton's slender Perpendicular tower. Do not miss
ne elaborate late 14th century font, the interesting
ssortment of carved corbel figures, nor the old alms
nest.

It is apparently still possible to walk northwards
or about a mile) to the ifamous Taynton stone
uarries (on Map 19). These have provided some of
ne finest stone in the whole Cotswolds, and material
om here was used in the building of St. Paul's
athedral, Blenheim Palace, and many of the Oxford
olleges.

JESTWELL

(20—NW) (2 miles South West of Burford)
delicious village with church, rectory and manor
ouse looking out across a rough green, complete with
ond. The impressively simple War Memorial incorpor-
tes a figure 'I', salvaged from the shattered Cloth Hall
t Ypres. The Norman church stands amongst fascinat-
ng tombs, and from the south porch, a path leads
owards the gorgeous rectory. Inside the church there
an attractive 17th century monument to the
rinder family, with husband, wife, six sons and
ght daughters all depicted.

VIDFORD

(20—NE) (1 mile East of Burford)
'alk across a field beyond the Windrush, and below
'idford Manor, to visit this delightfully unspoilt little
hurch, with its box pews, 14th century wall paintings
nd old stone floor incorporating part of a Roman
nosaic pavement (probably the floor of a villa on this
te).

Fettiplace Monument, Swinbrook

MAP 19 continued from P 91.

JESTCOTE

19—NW) (3½ miles South East of Stow-on-the-Wold)
mall village with gorgeous views eastwards over the
venlode valley to the distant, wooded heights of
'ychwood Forest. There is a 16th century manor
ouse and several pleasant old houses, but the church
the result of several 19th and 20th century re-builds,
nd is not of great interest to visitors. There is the
culptured base of a 15th century cross in the church-
ard, which was colourful with primroses and daffodils
hen we last called here.

The Rectory, Westwell

97

MAP 20

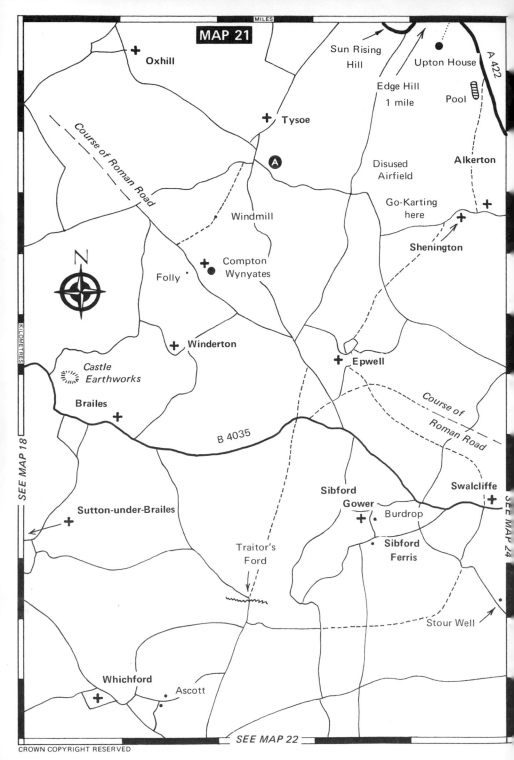

MAP 21

MILES

Oxhill

Sun Rising Hill

Upton House

A 422

Edge Hill
1 mile

Pool

Tysoe

Alkerton

A

Disused
Airfield

Windmill

Go-Karting
here

Shenington

Folly

Compton
Wynyates

N

Winderton

Epwell

Castle
Earthworks

Course of
Roman Road

Brailes

B 4035

Sibford
Gower

Swalcliffe

Burdrop

Sutton-under-Brailes

Sibford
Ferris

Traitor's
Ford

Stour Well

Whichford

Ascott

SEE MAP 18

SEE MAP 24

KILOMETRES

Course of Roman Road

SEE MAP 22

Map 21

Red Horse Country and the Northern Edge

BRAILES, COMPTON WYNYATES, THE SIBFORDS, UPTON HOUSE, etc. . . .

ALKERTON
(21—NE) (5 miles West of Banbury)
Looks across a deep valley to Shenington. Within the little church there is a real flavour of medieval times, with steps ascending from the nave to the chancel beneath the tower crossing. Do not overlook the 14th century carvings around the outside cornice to the south aisle, with men and dogs, and a bear amongst the figures.

ASCOTT
(21 SW) (5 miles North of Chipping Norton)
Pleasant hamlet below the hills near Whichford We liked the small metal horses on the gate pillars of attractive Vernon House.

House below the church, Alkerton

BRAILES
(21—SW) (8 miles North of Chipping Norton)
Upper and Lower Brailes, strung out along the B 4035, make up a village of considerable size There are several pleasant stone houses and a homely 16th century inn, the George Brailes church has a splendid Perpendicular tower, but by comparison, an unexciting interior. However do not miss the elaborately carved 14th century font. On a small hill to the immediate south are the earthworks of a medieval castle, probably built by one of the Earls of Warwick.

BURDROP
(21—SE) (6 miles West of Banbury)
Hamlet sandwiched between the two Sibfords (P 100) with a colourful little inn called the Bishop's Blaize looking out over a quiet valley running south west towards the Stour.

COMPTON WYNYATES
(21—NW) (8 miles West of Banbury)
A delightful Tudor mansion of mellow brick in a lovely setting amongst wooded hillsides. The unusual occurrence of brick in this stone countryside is probably accounted for by King Henry VIII's gift to Sir William Compton, of the ruined castle of Fulbroke, near Warwick, and Sir William's subsequent use of the salvaged materials at Compton.

The moat was filled in at the end of the Civil War and the famous clipped yews that used to adorn the gardens have now been removed. Compton Wynyates is, alas, no longer open to the public, but there are enchanting glimpses of it down from the road, and despite the removal of the yews, it remains one of the most beautifully sited English country houses.

Brailes Church

It is also possible to walk up to the restored windmill (not open), starting from a tree-lined track off the road well to the north of the house

EDGE HILL

(North of Map 21) (7 miles North West of Banbury)
Here, above the site of the Battle of Edge Hill, is the Castle Inn, a Gothick 'castle' built in 1749 by Sanderson Miller, squire of Radway, and gentleman architect extraordinary. From the 'Castle', a path leads through glorious woodlands and down fields to Radway, with views of Miller's Radway Grange.

EPWELL

Ford At Epwell

(21—NE) (6 miles West of Banbury)
An unassuming, Hornton stone village tucked away in a hollow, with a small ford just beyond a row of cottages, one of which used to be the Three Horseshoes Inn. The church has a small central tower, a thin Jacobean pulpit, a pleasing Perpendicular roof, and a pretty little 14th century piscina.

OXHILL

(21—NW) (9 miles North West of Banbury)
A stone village in the 'Vale of Red Horse' with a small, attractively signed inn, the Peacock; and an interesting, largely Norman church, looking out eastwards to the hilly scarp where the Red Horse was once in view (see Tysoe, P 101). Both north and south doorways are Norman, but the south one is a much richer specimen. There is a fine 15th century roof to the nave, and a fascinating Norman font, with the scrawny figures of Adam and Eve, at the 'Tree of Life'.

Cottages at Epwell   *Trophy Sign, Shenington*

SHENINGTON

(21—NE) (5 miles West of Banbury)
Large stone and thatch village, grouped around a wide green, and standing over five hundred feet above sea level. It has an attractive little inn, The Bell, and together with Alkerton has won Oxfordshire's Best Kept Village Trophy at least once. The interior of the church is all shiny tiles, pitch pine pews and scraped walls, but we liked the ornamentation of the south aisle arcade capitals, and the sculptured figures of a man and an ox on the outside south wall.

Shenington Church

SIBFORD FERRIS and SIBFORD GOWER

(21—SE) (6 miles West of Banbury)
Together with Burdrop (P 99) these two make up a large straggling village, with Ferris to the south of, and Gower to the north of, a quiet valley running southwestwards to the Stour. Ferris has a large Quaker boarding school including one or two elegant 18th century houses, and a short, unfenced road with fine views, leading south-westwards. Gower has an unremarkable Victorian church, many attractive stone and thatch cottages and a hospitable inn called the Wykeham Arms (this provides an enjoyable cold buffet).

STOUR WELL

(21—SE) (6 miles South West of Banbury)
This is in fact an uninspiring stone trough, but we include it because the road here is through open country, and there are splendid open views westwards

The Wykeham Arms, Sibford Gower

MAP 21   100

down the head of the Stour valley and over to the high Cotswolds (Broadway Tower visible through binoculars). This is watershed country with the Stour flowing west and north to the Avon, and almost all other streams flowing east and south to the Cherwell, and ultimately to the Thames.

SUNRISING HILL
(21—NE) (7 miles North West of Banbury)
One of the steepest main road hills in southern England. There are fine views out over the Vale of Red Horse for those not having to concentrate on the road, and there is a pleasant path north-eastwards through the woods to Edge Hill (P 100).

SUTTON-UNDER-BRAILES
(21—SW) (7 miles North of Chipping Norton)
Most of the village is spread around a delightful green, once shaded by lofty trees, but now having to 'start again', due to the ravages of Dutch elm disease in the 1970's. The church has a well proportioned south tower but the austere interior appears to have never recovered from restoration in the 1870's.

The Castle Inn, Edge Hill

Wall Paintings, Swalcliffe

SWALCLIFFE
(21—SE) (5 miles West of Banbury)
Has a massive tithe barn at its western end, said to have been built by the great William of Wykeham (see Broughton, P 112). At the centre of the village is a pleasant thatched inn, called the Stag's Head (fondly remembered for its bread and cheese), which is overlooked from the other side of the road by the church. This has a handsome 17th century door within a 'Decorated' style south doorway, and an old roof looking down on pleasing 17th century seating, pulpit and lectern, and colourful monuments of the same period. Don't miss the wall paintings.

Wall Monument, Swalcliffe

TRAITOR'S FORD
(21—SW) (6 miles North of Chipping Norton)
A beautifully cool place in the lightly wooded upper Stour valley (it could be crowded on Sunday afternoons). Who was, or who were, the traitor(s)? We know not, but always imagine a small but bloody encounter involving feudal retainers. An old bridle-way (Ditchedge Lane) leads north from here.

TYSOE
(21—NW and NE) (8 miles North West of Banbury)
A long straggle of Upper, Middle and Lower Tysoe, beneath the scarp face on which the Red Horse was once carved. This has long since disappeared, and much of the hillside has been planted with soft woods in recent years. There is much modern development, but the little 'old' fire station, with its thatched roof, still stands next to the Peacock Inn, which ironically was largely destroyed by fire some years ago.

The Interior of the church is rather cold, with scraped and pointed walls, but there is a fine 14th century font, with figures beneath crocketed canopies, some medieval and Jacobean seating, and three interesting brasses.

Traitor's Ford

UPTON HOUSE see P 122.

WHICHFORD see P 122.

WINDERTON see P 122.

Edge Country near Tysoe — Map Ref Ⓐ

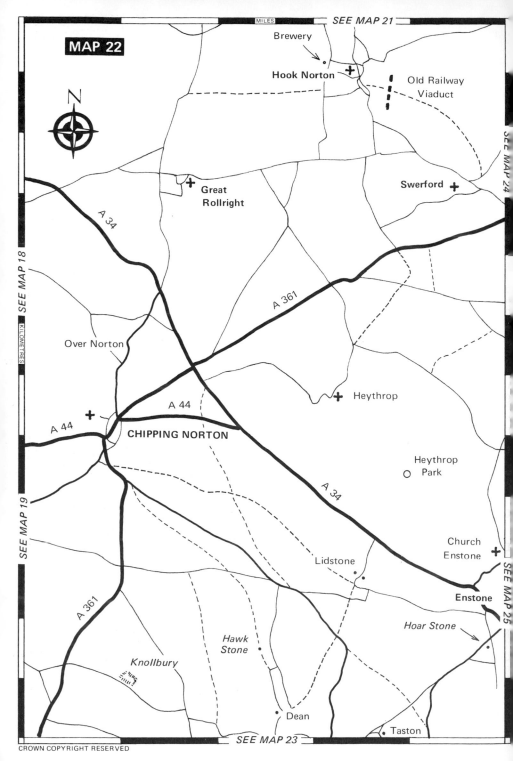

MAP 22

MILES

Brewery

Hook Norton

Old Railway
Viaduct

N

Great
Rollright

Swerford

A 34

A 361

KILOMETRES

Over Norton

Heythrop

A 44

A 44

CHIPPING NORTON

Heythrop
Park

A 34

Church
Enstone

Lidstone

Enstone

A 361

Hoar Stone

Hawk
Stone

Knollbury

Dean

Taston

Map 22

Heythrop Country and the Nortons

CHIPPING NORTON, GREAT ROLLRIGHT, HEYTHROP, HOOK NORTON, etc. . . .

CHIPPING NORTON

(22—SW) (12 miles South West of Banbury)
Busy Cotswold market town, where tourism has never been allowed to overshadow the everyday lives of those who live and work here. It is built on west facing slopes with a large Victorian tweed mill in the valley, still looking less at home here than in some darker, deeper valley in Yorkshire's West Riding. The long Market Square (or Chepynge, as it was called in medieval times.....hence Chipping) is dominated by the handsome 19th century Town Hall, and is overlooked by pleasant 17th, 18th and 19th century hotels, inns and shops (we recall the hospitality of the White Hart with particular pleasure).

There are a row of quaint almshouses (built 1640) on the cul-de-sac road down to the church. This lies in the valley bottom, to the immediate south of the earthworks of a large medieval castle. The largely Perpendicular church, no doubt built mainly with money amassed in the wool trade, has an unusual polygonal porch, with a vaulted ceiling, but its interior has been disappointingly over-restored by the Victorians, and lacks much feeling of antiquity. The interesting series of brasses have been mounted on wooden plaques, further emphasing this point, but the handsome tombs of Richard Croft and Thomas Rickardes, should not be overlooked.

Chipping Norton Church *Antiques at Chipping Norton*

17th Century Almshouses, Chipping Norton

CHURCH ENSTONE

(22—SE) (see Enstone below)

DEAN

(22—SE) (3 miles South East of Chipping Norton)
Unspoilt hamlet on the upper slopes of a small valley running south to the Evenlode. There is a fine manor house amongst trees above the road and a bridle-way north north-east across high downland country to Lidstone (P 105).

ENSTONE

(22—SE) (4 miles South East of Chipping Norton)
Church Enstone and Neat Enstone face each other across the valley of the little River Glyme. The old Litchfield Arms in Neat Enstone, once a coaching inn on the busy Oxford road, is now no more. To Enstone once came fashionable visitors to 'Queen Henrietta's Waterworks', a grotto with springs, waterfalls, a banquet hall, and the inevitable hired 'hermit', This was established here in 1636 and survived with varying fortunes until the close of the 18th century. Sadly

Dean Hamlet

Great Rollright Church

there is now no trace of these 'famous wells...etc' described by the diarist John Evelyn in 1664.

Traffic now thunders through Neat Enstone, but fortunately Church Enstone lies well away from the busy A 34. It is prettily sited on slopes above the Glyme valley, with an attractive inn called the Crown (snacks and meals at the bar), and a little road lined with cottages leading up to the church. This has retained its character well, and is full of interest. See especially the fine Norman south doorway, the 15th century porch and the touching monument to Steven Wisdom in the south aisle.

GREAT ROLLRIGHT
(22—NW) (2½ miles North of Chipping Norton)
Exposed upland village with no real features of interest apart from its Norman church. This has some grotesque gargoyles on its well proportioned Perpendicular tower and a Norman doorway whose tympanum has a fish inserted amongst various geometric carvings. Inside there is ample evidence of those Victorian restorers but do not miss the brass to John Battersby, rector here until his death in 1522; nor the pleasant roof with the names of churchwardens in 1814 on one of its beams.

Tympanum at Great Rollright

THE HAWK STONE
(22—SW) (2½ miles South East of Chipping Norton)
An isolated eight foot high sarsen stone standing in a field a short distance to the west of the road running north from Dean hamlet. Is it the sole survivor of a long barrow's burial chamber? No one appears to know the answer, but it stands in pleasant countryside, with views across to Knollbury.

HEYTHROP
(22—SE) (2½ miles East of Chipping Norton)
There is a pleasant open road from the A 34 near Chipping Norton to the minute estate village of Heythrop, ending in an avenue of trees leading to a splendidly towered Victorian church (see the pleasant stone reredos depicting the Last Supper). Beside it, on private ground, stands the chancel of a little Norman church, with its chancel arch now serving as a west doorway. There are fine views out over Heythrop Park, which was laid out by Charles Talbot, Duke of Shrewsbury in the 18th century, and which is nearly four miles long. Talbot's mansion, built by Thomas Archer, was destroyed by fire in the 1830's and was not re-built until forty years later. Until recently it was a Jesuit seminary, but it is now a Staff College run by the National Westminster Bank. It is neither open to the public, nor visible from any road.

Heythrop Church

THE HOAR STONE
(22—SE) (4 miles South East of Chipping Norton)
In fact there are three great stones, the largest nine feet high, which are the remains of a stone age burial chamber (about 2000 BC). They stand in bushes by a cross road half a mile to the south of Enstone, where the road from there to Ditchley crosses the B 4022

The Hoar Stone, near Enstone

MAP 22   104

HOOK NORTON

(22—NE) (5 miles North East of Chipping Norton)
A large village which is full of character and interest.
There is a Victorian brewery and the dramatic piers of
a dismantled railway viaduct which used to span the
broad valley to the east.....evidence of 'Hooky's' past
importance as a source of ironstone. 'The Green' and
'East End' are both very pleasant, but we particularly
liked the terrace in the centre of the village looking
southwards, with the Bell Inn at one end and the
church at the other. The latter is a large building with
a finely pinnacled Perpendicular tower and a spacious
interior whose contents include a fascinating ; Norman
font complete with Adam and Eve, and Sagittarius the
Archer (a favourite subject in this area. (See Salford,
P. 87 and Kencot, P 96.)

Font,
Hook Norton

Memorial at
Over Norton

KNOLLBURY

(22—SW) (2½ miles South of Chipping Norton)
A pronounced rectangular earthwork of uncertain
origin, in open country to the immediate north of the
Sarsden—Chadlington road. There are fine downland
views eastwards.

LIDSTONE

(22 SE) (3 miles South East of Chipping Norton)
Hamlet on the steep southern slopes of the Glyme
valley. The little Talbot Arms is no more, and there is
now no special reason to visit Lidstone. However the
situation is one which we covet.....looking out across
to the woods of Heythrop Park, and well removed
from the busy A 34.

Viaduct Piers near Hook Norton

OVER NORTON

(22—NW) (1 mile North of Chipping Norton)
Pretty hamlet on the edge of a fine, wooded park,
with a fascinating three legged Victorian memorial
situated on a little green just below the road. Too close
to Chipping Norton to have any real identity of its own.

TASTON

(22—SE) (4 miles South East of Chipping Norton)
Small hamlet with the interesting base of a 14th century wayside cross, and a minute stream beside the road
in a little valley below.

Lidstone Hamlet

SWERFORD

(22 NE) (5 miles North East of Chipping Norton)
Situated near the head of the quiet valley of the Swere,
which flows east from here to join the Cherwell near
Deddington. Swerford has a pleasant green by the
church, which is set in a neat churchyard overlooking
the earthworks of a long vanished Norman castle, and
has a dumpy spire and a 13th century porch enriched
with a series of earthy gargoyles. The interior is not
very exciting.

There is a delightful, but all too short, field road
over towards Wiggington (P 122), with glimpses of the
Swere to its immediate south.

Taston Cross

MAP 22

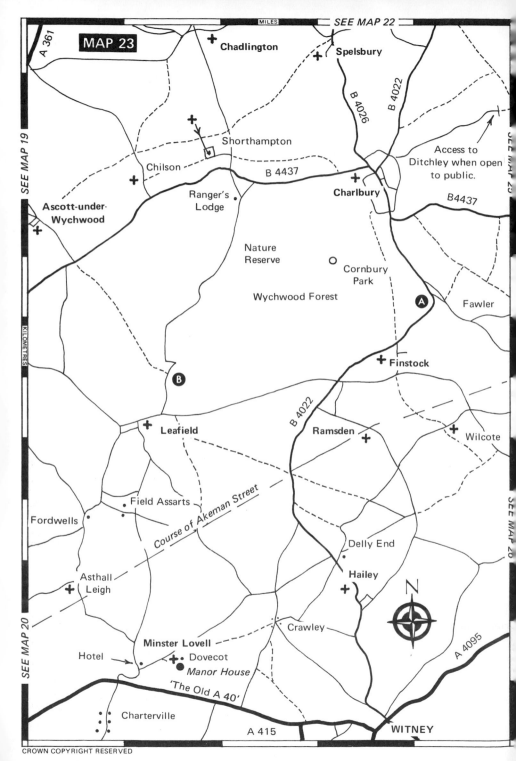

MAP 23

A 361

SEE MAP 19

SEE MAP 22

Chadlington

Spelsbury

B 4026

B 4022

Shorthampton

Chilson

B 4437

Charlbury

Access to
Ditchley when open
to public.

SEE MAP 25

B4437

Ranger's
Lodge

Ascott-under-
Wychwood

Nature
Reserve

Cornbury
Park

Wychwood Forest

Fawler

A

KILOMETRES

Finstock

B

B 4022

Ramsden

Wilcote

Leafield

Field Assarts

Course of Akeman Street

Fordwells

Delly End

Asthall
Leigh

Hailey

N

SEE MAP 20

Crawley

Minster Lovell

Hotel

Dovecot

Manor House

'The Old A 40'

A 4095

SEE MAP 20

Charterville

A 415

WITNEY

MILES

Map 23

Wychwood Country and the Lower Windrush

CHARLBURY, LEAFIELD, MINSTER LOVELL, WITNEY, etc. . . .

ASCOTT-UNDER-WYCHWOOD

(23—NW) (5 miles North East of Burford)
Long straggling village in the lush Evenlode valley
with a railway still making its mark on the landscape.
This is the old GWR, Paddington to Worcester line,
which keeps the Evenlode company all the way from its
confluence with the Glyme near Bladon, almost up to
its source near Moreton-in-Marsh. There are two pubs
including the prettily signed Swan Inn, a very crisply
converted mill house and a partly Norman church. This
sits in a large churchyard, with converging avenues of
lime trees, and is overlooked by old stone houses on
all four sides. The interior has all been rather tidied up,
but there is Norman arcading to the north aisle and a
handsome triple sedilia beneath one of the chancel
windows.

Ascott-under-Wychwood Church

ASTHALL LEIGH

(23—SW) (3 miles North West of Witney)
Small upland village looking south across the Windrush
valley towards the distant line of the Berkshire Downs.
The Old Crown Inn no longer offers refreshment, and is
now entitled 'Old Crown Cottage'. The Victorian
church appears to be of little interest to visitors.

CHADLINGTON

(23—NW) (2 miles North West of Charlbury)
A long village looking south over the Evenlode valley
towards Wychwood Forest. it has no fewer than three
inns (The Malt Shovel, the Sandys Arms, and the Tite
Inn), together with a pleasant old manor house, and
substantial church, enriched with a multitude of
fascinating gargoyles. It has a clerestory, a rich series
of corbel figures, and is generally well cared for, but it
is rather lacking in atmosphere. There are fine walks
northwards over the farmlands of Chadlington Downs
(see the Hawk Stone, P 104).

Chadlington Manor

CHARLBURY

(23 NE) (6 miles North of Witney)
Small town, tucked away in the Evenlode valley,
enviably far from the busy main roads. Charlbury looks
across the valley to the 600 acre Cornbury Park, which
is backed by the great woodlands of Wychwood Forest.
Commuting Oxonians have brought fresh life to Charlbury, but it retains a most agreeable rural flavour, not
least in its assortment of appetising inns.

The mainly Perpendicular church is not exceptional,
but it blends in well with the stone fronted houses,
shops and inns that constitute this pleasant town.

The Bell Hotel, Charlbury

The Green, Delly End

Mill House, near Finstock — Map Ref.

Leafield Church   *Leafield Cross*

Cottages at Leafield

CHARTERVILLE

(23—SW) (3 miles West of Witne
Nearly three hundred acres lying each side of the roa
here were purchased by one of the Chartists in 184
and were then split up into small holdings. These we
handed over to poor families from the industr
towns, already ploughed, and endowed with thir
pounds and a pig. But sadly, like so many ideal
enterprises, it soon foundered. One or two of the litt
bungalows remain unaltered, but most have bee
smartened up beyond easy recognition and now appe
to a casual observer to be the dwellings of independe
folk who might not be entirely in sympathy with th
liberal ideals that lead to their construction. A
rather sad.

CHILSON

(23—NW) (2½ miles West of Charlbur
Hamlet on the southern slopes of the Evenlode vall
with attractive stone farmhouses and cottages.

CORNBURY PARK

(23—NE) (1 mile South West of Charlbur
A magnificent six hundred acre deer park with gre
avenues of trees and a chain of lakes, occupying t
north eastern sector of Wychwood Forest (P 122
Cornbury House is a splendid 17th century mansio
which stemmed from an earlier hunting lodge. Charl
II's Lord Chancellor, the Earl of Clarendon started wor
on his great History of the Great Rebellion her
although he was exiled to France long before its cor
pletion. Mouth watering glimpses of diarist. Joh
Evelyn's 'sweete parke'* are obtainable from the gat
to the south west of Charlbury, but there is no gener
access granted to the public by the present owne
* Not of course owned by Evelyn.

CRAWLEY

(23—SE) (1½ miles North West of Witne
Has a pleasant inn, the Lamb, and a few farms ar
cottages looking down on its small stream, and an o
blanket mill on the Windrush a short distance sout

DELLY END

(23—SE) (2 miles North of Witne
Beautiful hamlet grouped around a well mown gree
complete with a domed memorial on four slend
columns, and overlooked by a series of delectable sto
houses.

FAWLER

(23—NE) (2 miles South East of Charlbur
Hamlet close to the Evenlode with a substantial farr
and pleasant footpaths across to Finstock and Wilcot

FINSTOCK

(23—NE) (2 miles South of Charlbury
Described by John Wesley, who visited it three time
(1774-7-8), as 'this delightful solitude', its inhabitants being
'a plain and artless people' (no doubt a compliment coming
from J.W.). Finstock today is a fragmented village, with a
fine gabled manor house and a plain Victorian church.

FORDWELLS

(23—SW) (4 miles North West of Witney
This hamlet is attractively sited in the valley of a sma
stream flowing south to the Windrush.

MAP 23   108

AILEY
(23–SE) (2 miles North of Witney)
n unexceptional stone village astride the B 4022, with
Victorian church of no great interest to visitors.

EAFIELD
(23–SW) (4 miles North West of Witney)
his long straggling village stands on high ground
tween the Evenlode and Windrush valleys, and just to
e south west of Wychwood Forest (in medieval
mes it must have stood near the forest's centre).
he tall spired church was the work of Sir Gilbert
ott (1860), and has an austere but rather grand
terior. It looks out across a long green, with a med-
val cross, which was restored by the villagers in 1873
thanks for its 'deliverance from the scourge of
mallpox'. There are fine views southwards, three inns,
d a bevy of ugly radio masts not far away.

Manor and Church at Minster Lovell

INSTER LOVELL
(23–SW) (2½ miles West of Witney)
he ruined 15th century manor house of the Lovells is
mantically sited on the willow bordered banks of the
ndrush. Do not overlook the circular dovecot, nor
e fine cruciform church, with its vaulted central
ossing. The village itself is perhaps rather self-consci-
sly trim, but it is good to see the buildings so well
aintained. There is a delightful little hotel here... the
d Swan.

AMSDEN
(23–SE) (3 miles North of Witney)
easant village on the line of the Akeman Street (P 61).
s cross roads are marked by an unusual stone war
emorial, and this is overlooked by the Royal Oak,
d an attractive row of cottages.....all in Cotswold
one. The church is Victorian and not of great
terest.

Ramsden

HORTHAMPTON
(23–NW) (2 miles West of Charlbury)
quiet hamlet overlooking the Evenlode valley, with
farm, a few cottages and an unspoilt little medieval
urch. This was overlooked by those over zealous
ictorians, and its high backed pews and two decker
ulpit (all 18th century work) have survived intact.
here is also a most interesting series of wall paintings
the 15th, 16th and 17th centuries.

'Young Farmers' at Wilcote

PELSBURY
(23–NE) (1½ miles North of Charlbury)
n unpretentious village with a pleasant blending of
one and thatch, a row of gabled almshouses and a
ne church looking out over the Evenlode valley. This
as a grand tower and a series of splendid monuments
the Lee family (latterly the Earls of Litchfield) of
arby Ditchley Park (P 115). Do not miss this.

ILCOTE
(23–SE) (3 miles South East of Charlbury)
deliciously quiet, tree shaded hamlet, with large
uses withdrawn from the road, and a small, partly
orman church, with little of interest to show.

ITNEY see P 122.

YCHWOOD FOREST   see P 122.

The Edge of Wychwood Forest – Map Ref.

MAP 23

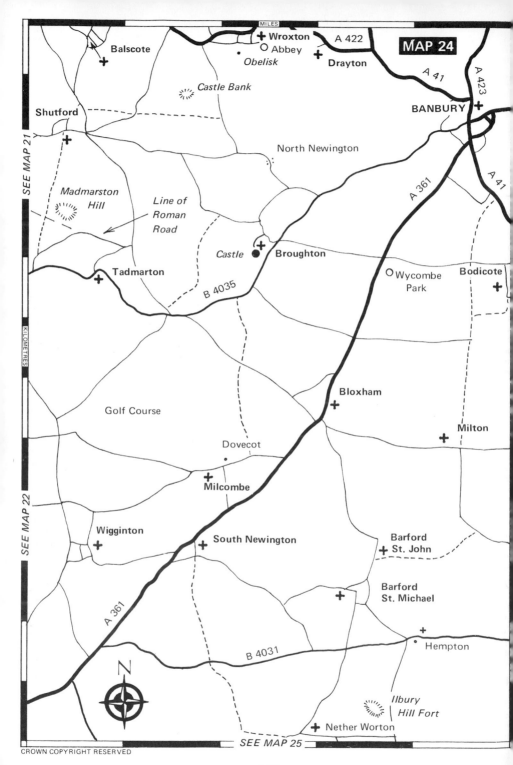

MILES

MAP 24

A 422

A 41

A 423

✝ **Wroxton**
○ **Abbey**
Obelisk

✝ **Drayton**

Balscote
✝

Castle Bank

BANBURY ✝

Shutford
✝

SEE MAP 21

North Newington

A 361

A 41

Madmarston Hill

Line of Roman Road

✝ **Castle** ● **Broughton**

Tadmarton
✝

KILOMETRES

B 4035

○ **Wycombe Park**

Bodicote
✝

Golf Course

Bloxham
✝

Milton
✝

Dovecot

Milcombe
✝

SEE MAP 22

Wigginton
✝

South Newington
✝

Barford St. John
✝

Barford St. Michael
✝

A 361

Hempton
✝

B 4031

Ilbury Hill Fort

N

✝ **Nether Worton**

SEE MAP 25

Map 24

Ironstone Country of the Far North East

BANBURY, BLOXHAM, BROUGHTON CASTLE, THE NEWINGTONS, WROXTON, etc. . . .

ALSCOTE
(24—NW) (4 miles West of Banbury)
, minute village, undisturbed by the ironstone work-
ngs nearby. Consists of a few farms, and cottages, the
utchers Arms, and a 14th century church on a wood-
d knoll.

ANBURY
(24—NE) (12 miles North East of Chipping Norton)
or centuries Banbury has been a busy market town,
nd it is now steadily growing in importance as an
ndustrial centre. Despite much 're development' it still
as a few old alleys and quiet corners, and the old
anal wharf is now busy again during the summer with
aft using the Oxford Canal.....one of the loveliest in
e country.

Banbury Cross is a mid 19th century replacement
f a medieval cross destroyed by the Puritans in the
rly 17th century, and the handsome late 18th cent-
ry church was built by S.P. Cockerell, the architect
f Daylesford (P 89) and Sezincote (P 72), to replace
medieval building which the citizens of Banbury had
ound necessary to destroy with gunpowder. Recent
evelopments in the centre of the town are not without
eir critics. However we do not suggest that the citi-
ens resort to a similar solution in an endeavour to
ease.

Banbury Church   Bloxham Spire

ARFORD ST. JOHN
(24—SE) (5 miles South of Banbury)
aces Barford St. Michael across the little Swere
alley. Its small church lies behind a farmyard, and
though heavily restored, possesses a good Norman
oorway.

Thorneycroft Monument, Bloxham

ARFORD ST. MICHAEL
(24—SE) (5 miles South of Banbury)
he squat Norman church looks out across the Swere
alley from its Norman north doorway. This doorway
one of Oxfordshire's outstanding art treasures, with
antastic carvings of beak heads and chevrons, and
tertwining decoration on capitals and tympanum.
lease spare time to look at this magnificent work.

LOXHAM
(24—SE) (4 miles South West of Banbury)
large village strung out along the A 361, Bloxham has
strong enough character to overcome this disadvant-
ge. Its well built stone houses, cottages and inns are
ted on a multitude of different levels.
At the Banbury end of the village, stands Bloxham

North Doorway, Barford St. Michael

School, most of which was designed by G.E. Street However the focal point of Bloxham is its magnificen 14th century church spire, which soars to a height o almost 200 feet. The church below is of considerabl scale, and is well worth visiting. It has an attractiv south doorway, and some fascinating medieval ston figures, beneath the tower parapet, and high up in th north aisle. See also the very grand 18th century tom of Sir John Thorneycroft.

BODICOTE

(24—NE) (2 miles South of Banbury
Bodicote might so easily have become a suburb o Banbury, but although it is perhaps less rural tha villages further west or south, it has retained a charac ter of its own. There are several elegant house (especially in East Street), some thatched cottages and no fewer than three inns.....the Horse and Jockey the Plough and the Baker's Arms. The largely Per pendicular church stands at the south western edg of the village, but its interior is not of great interest t visitors.

Doorway at Bodicote   *Broughton Church*

Castle and Church at Broughton

BROUGHTON CASTLE and BROUGHTON

(24—NW) (3 miles South West of Banbury
Built in 1306, Broughton Castle is the home of Lor Saye and Sele, whose ancestor, the Second Baro acquired it by marriage to the heiress of William o Wykeham, founder of Winchester and New College Oxford. In the 16th century a beautiful 'Elizabethan front was added and, many interior improvement carried out, but this has not disturbed Broughton' extraordinarily strong atmosphere. Viewed from th park across its reedy moat, the castle reveals itself a one of Oxfordshire's most romantic buildings.

The adjoining church has a fine chancel screen an a splendid series of monuments, and should certainl not be overlooked.

DRAYTON

(24—NE) (2 miles West of Banbury
Small village astride the curving A 422, with an in called the Roebuck and a largely 14th century churc lying by itself in a hollow, looking across to Wroxtor Abbey's parklands. It has a truncated tower, an earl priest's doorway, and the effigies of two 15th century knights, John and Ludovic Greville, the latter i company with his lady.

Effigies in Broughton Church

HEMPTON

(24—SE) (5½ miles South of Banbury
A stone and thatch hamlet spread out along the hig B 4031, with views northwards out over the Swer (rather spoilt by the cat's cradle of radio aerials on th hill beyond). The small Victorian church has a Norma font with chevron decoration, but little else of interes to visitors.

MADMARSTON HILL

(24—NW) (5 miles West of Banbury
Site of an Iron Age hill fort, with the line of a Roma road at its foot, which ran from Droitwich, throug Alcester and Stratford, past Madmarston toward King's Sutton. Evidence of an extensive Romano British settlement has been unearthed to the south east of the hill.

The Gatehouse, Broughton Castle

MAP 24

112

MILCOMBE
(24—SW) (5 miles South West of Banbury)
An undistinguished village with a small church which, apart from its tower, was re-built by the Victorians. However do not miss the very handsome octagonal dovecot, with its lantern top and four dormer windows.

MILTON
(24—SE) (3½ miles South of Banbury)
Quiet 'tucked-away' little village with a hospitable inn called the Black Boy, next door to the Victorian church, a small but elegant building by the great Victorian architect, William Butterfield (best known for Keble College, Oxford). There is a monstrous car pump a short distance to the west.

Dovecot at Milcombe

Doorway at Wigginton

NETHER WORTON
(24—SE) (6½ miles South of Banbury)
An immaculate farm, a very grand manor house, and minute church with deserted schoolroom attached. This and a few cottages make up Nether Worton, a deliciously quiet hamlet sheltering beneath wooded Hawk Hill.

NORTH NEWINGTON
(24—NW) (2 miles West of Banbury)
An unexceptional hamlet overlooking the valley below Wroxton Abbey park, with two inns, the Baker's Arms and the Roebuck, the latter looking very colourful.

SHUTFORD
(24—NW) (4½ miles West of Banbury)
Quiet village amidst small bumpy hills. The prettily signed George and Dragon inn is comfortably sited almost beneath the church. This has a miniature, pinnacled tower, Norman arcading, a pleasant oak screen and early 19th century box pews. There is a bridle-path south from here to Swalcliffe (P 101)

Nether Worton Church

SOUTH NEWINGTON
(24—NW) (6 miles South West of Banbury)
Delightful village on the River Swere, with an inn on the main road called the Wykeham Arms. Much of the rest of the village lies beyond a small trim green, which is overlooked by South Newington's exceptionally interesting church. This has a handsome Perpendicular porch with canopied niche, a cylindrical Norman font, a Jacobean pulpit, and a series of box pews (all as originally numbered, which is an unusual survival in these parts). However most visitors come here to see the splendid series of 14th century wall paintings... a wonderful picture-book bible for the medieval peasants of this parish, and fascinating in its detail. Do not overlook the framed documents relating to compulsory burial in woollen shrouds...a once popular measure in this sheep country.

South Newington

TADMARTON
(24—NW) (4 miles South West of Banbury)
Modest stone and thatch village strung out along the B 4035, with a handsome manor house opposite the church. Do not miss the fine 14th century font, with its richly detailed ornamentation.

WIGGINTON see P 122.

WROXTON see P 122.

Wroxton Village Pond

MAP 24

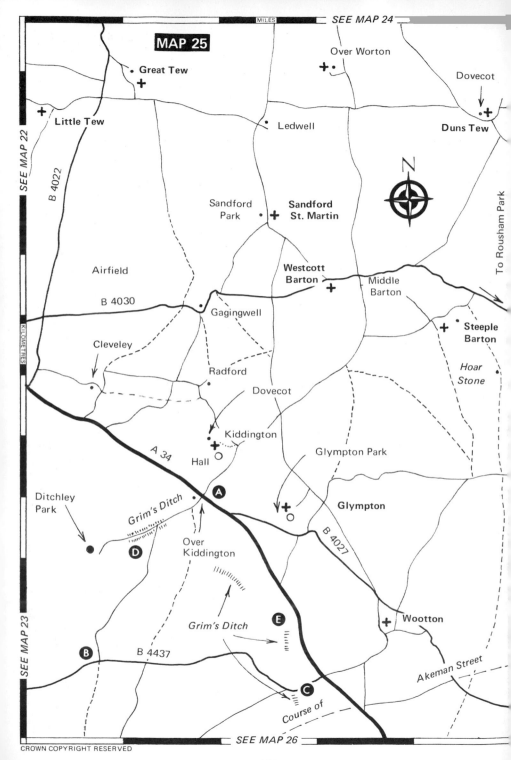

MAP 25

MILES

Great Tew

Over Worton

Dovecot

Little Tew

Ledwell

Duns Tew

B 4022

Sandford
Park

Sandford
St. Martin

N

To Rousham Park

Airfield

B 4030

Westcott
Barton

Middle
Barton

Gagingwell

Steeple
Barton

Cleveley

KILOMETRES

Radford

Hoar
Stone

Dovecot

Kiddington

A 34

Hall

Glympton Park

Ditchley
Park

Grim's Ditch

Glympton

B 4027

Over
Kiddington

D

SEE MAP 23

B

Grim's Ditch

B 4437

E

Wootton

C

Akeman Street

Course of

Map 25

Tewland and the Glyme Valley

DITCHLEY PARK, ROUSHAM PARK, SANDFORD ST. MARTIN, THE TEWS, etc. . . .

LEVELEY

(25—SW) (5 miles South East of Chipping Norton)
uiet hamlet on the sides of a steep cleft in the upper
lyme valley, with no special features apart from its
ither dramatic site. There is a footpath down the
illey to Radford Bridge (P 117).

DITCHLEY PARK

(25—SW) (4½ miles North West of Woodstock)
splendid mansion in a three hundred acre park,
omplete with lake, temples and woodlands. The house
·as designed by James Gibbs, the architect of St.
lartin in the Fields, in the 1770's, with interior
ecorations by William Kent. Ditchley was the week-
nd headquarters of Winston Churchill in the 39—45
·ar, and it is now a conference centre. (See opening
mes.) Approach from Charlbury or Over Kiddington.
There is an attractive open road between Over
.iddington on A 34 (Map ref. **A**) and B 4437 about
·vo miles east of Charlbury (Map ref **B**).

DUNS TEW

(25—NE) (7 miles North of Woodstock)
 tidy stone and thatch village with a character inn
alled the White Horse, and a delicious circular dovecot,
/hich was gay with climbing roses when we passed this
vay. The church, with its large squat tower, stands
eside a fine manor house, in a rose decked church-
ard with two pretty, early 19th century tombstones
ear the south door. The interior was over restored
nd is not of great interest apart from some sculptured
igures on corbels and arcade capitals.

SAGINGWELL

(25—NW) (5½ miles North West of Woodstock)
leasant hamlet on B 4030, with a small stream
.inning south towards Radford (P 117), and the rather
ninspiring base of a medieval wayside cross.

GLYMPTON

(25—SE) (3 miles North of Woodstock)
Much money has been spent on this recently built
Cotswold' village, which is already mellowing satisfac-
orily. The Glyme tumbles over a small waterfall by
he bridge.....a lovely, cool place in high summer.
The church lies behind the great house in lush
ilympton Park, and the delightful walk amply justifies
 visit. See the splendid tomb of Thomas Teesdale,
vool trader and benefactor of Balliol and Pembroke
olleges.

South Porch, Duns Tew   Dovecot at Duns Tew

Glympton Park

Monument at Glympton

Stocks at Great Tew

Hopcrofts Holt Hotel

Dovecot at Kiddington

Below Kiddington Bridge

GREAT TEW

(25—NW) (5½ miles East of Chipping Nortc
A 'model' village constructed by the early 19th cer
ury landscape gardener, John Loudon, as part of
extensive park overlooking the Worton valley. Her
the unusual number of evergreens in 'Tewland'. The
are 'picturesque' stone cottages, an inn and stocks
the village green; but it was planned so long ago, th
it not longer appears contrived.

The manor where Lord Falkland entertained poe
and philosophers from Oxford, has been replaced by
odd 19th century mansion, built by the descendar
of Matthew Boulton, partner of James Watt in t
famous Soho Foundry. Great Tew therefore owes
idyllic setting to Black Country sweat in the ear
years of the Industrial Revolution.

One of the Boultons, Mary, is remembered in t
church above the manor where there is a brillia
monument to her by Chantrey. The approach to t
church is up a delightful tree lined path, and t
attractive interior makes this walk worthwhile.

GRIM'S DITCH

(Map 2
A now disconnected series of banks and ditches, whi
were part of a defensive system built by Iron A
(Belgic) tribes in the first part of the 1st century A.I
The best sections are visible in Blenheim and Ditchl
Parks (see Map refs. **C** and **D**). and parallel with A
(see Map ref. **E**).

HOPCROFT'S HOLT

(Off Map 25) (1 mile East of Steeple Barto
A comfortable looking wayside hotel where legends
highwaymen persist. But the sordid truth points to t
murder of the inn keeper and his wife by a petty thie
one night in January 1754.....so much for the 'gent
men of the road'!

KIDDINGTON

(25—SW) (4 miles North West of Woodstoc
Here is a large stone mansion, Kiddington Park, ove
looking a landscaped lake in the Glyme valley. Th
little church is prettily sited beside the mansion, but
has been so heavily restored that very little atmosphe
remains. Do not overlook the beautifully roofed circ
lar dovecot just beyond the churchyard wall (do n
trespass beyond wall).

LEDWELL

(25—NE) (7 miles North of Woodstoc
Dignified little hamlet complete with Primitive Meth
dist chapel. Lord Deloraine, third son of the ill fate
Duke of Monmouth had a mansion here, but it h
long since vanished.

LITTLE TEW

(25—NW) (4 miles East of Chipping Norto
Small village is a wooded hollow, with a little saddl
back towered Victorian church.....interior not
interest to visitors. There are two pleasant old hous
at the western end of the village.

MIDDLE BARTON

(See Westcott Barton, P 122.)

MAP 25   116

VER WORTON

(25—NE) (7 miles South of Banbury)
here is a delightful open road between here and
ther Worton (P 113), overlooked by a Victorian
urch beautifully situated in a clump of trees. To
ach, the church, walk past thatched cottages in
lourful gardens, in front of a dignified late Georgian
anor, and pass the base of a medieval cross, which
arks the entry to Over Worton's quiet churchyard.
here are flowering trees and entrancing views out
er the bumpy wooded landscape from the church-
rd, but the church has no special features of interest.
o not overlook the beautiful little Georgian rectory
yond the churchyard path.

Rousham

ADFORD

(25—SW) (5 miles North West of Woodstock)
here is a pleasant open road, rather rough in places,
ove the little River Glyme, between Kiddington and
e hamlet of Radford. The willowy valley shelters a
all watermill, now put to other uses.

OUSHAM PARK

(Off Map 25) (2½ miles East of Middle Barton,
on B 4030)
cobean mansion enlarged and enriched by William
ent in 1738. While the house with its fine collection
portraits and furniture is of considerable interest, a
sit to its landscape gardens is a unique experience.

The only surviving example of Kent's landscape
sign, Rousham Gardens are sited along the rushy,
ee shaded banks of the Cherwell. Walking amongst
ese hanging woods, one comes across Italian Statuary.
arkling rivulets, and a lovely Classical summer house.

See also the lovely old flower borders in the walled
rden, the 16th century dovecot with revolving ladder,
d the church, with its Cottrell Dormer monuments.

Sandford Park

ANDFORD ST. MARTIN

(25—NE) (6 miles North of Woodstock)
elightful village of stone and thatch with a snug
anor house, and Sandford Park, a lovely 18th cent-
y mansion, with extensive gardens (not open to the
blic). Lord Deloraine (see Ledwell, P 116) is buried
the churchyard nearby.

TEEPLE BARTON

(25—NE) (5 miles North of Woodstock)
beautifully quiet place with a few houses and a
urch standing by itself at the end of a lane, overlook-
ng the parklands of Barton Abbey, a large house on a
te once owned by Oseney Abbey. There is no sign of
steeple here, but the stout Perpendicular tower dom-
ates the large sloping churchyard. The interior
ontains arcading ornamented with splendid medieval
eads of both men and beasts.

There is a bridle-way south from the church and
nother one starting out through the park, and which
ads all the way to Woodstock. This latter path passes
lose to the Hoar Stone, a long barrow in a wood near
arton Lodge, with a long mound and the chaotic
emains of its burial chamber.

Men and Beasts at Steeple Barton

WESTCOTT BARTON and MIDDLE BARTON
ee P 122.

WOOTTON see P 122.

By Wootton Bridge

MAP 25

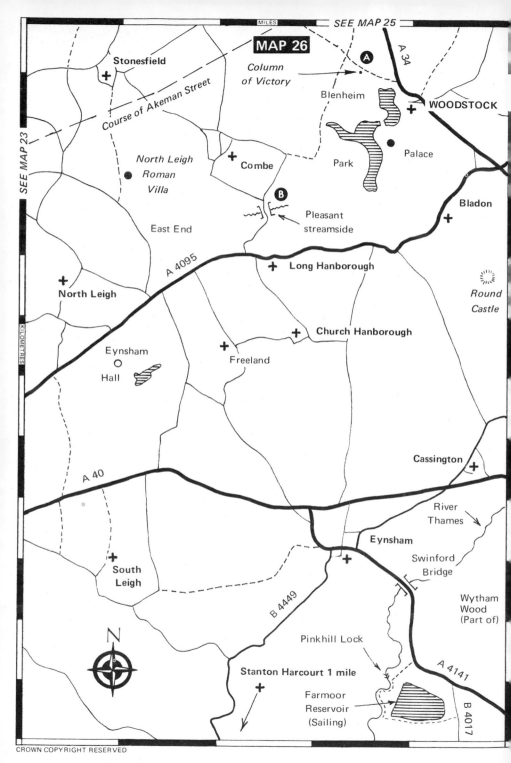

MILES

MAP 26

Stonesfield

Column
of Victory

A 34

Blenheim

WOODSTOCK

Course of Akeman Street

North Leigh
Roman
Villa

Combe

Park

Palace

East End

Pleasant
streamside

Bladon

A 4095

Long Hanborough

Round
Castle

North Leigh

KILOMETRES

Church Hanborough

Eynsham
Hall

Freeland

Cassington

A 40

River
Thames

Eynsham

Swinford
Bridge

South
Leigh

B 4449

Wytham
Wood
(Part of)

N

Pinkhill Lock

A 4141

Stanton Harcourt 1 mile

Farmoor
Reservoir
(Sailing)

B 4017

Map 26

The Churchill Country

BLADON, BLENHEIM PALACE, EYNSHAM, THE LEIGHS, WOODSTOCK, etc. . . .

BLADON

(26—NE) (1 mile South of Woodstock)
long village astride the A 4095, almost overshadowed by the great woodlands bordering Blenheim Park. Sir Winston Churchill lies in a simple grave in the church yard here. The circular earthwork, known as Round Castle, in woods to the south east are probably the remains of a medieval castle.

BLENHEIM PALACE

(26—NE) (To immediately South of Woodstock)
nce through the entrance gate, one is met by a pros ect of palace, bridge and a great lake, with sweeping anks, clad here and there with noble woodlands. This the work of Vanbrugh and Capability Brown brought o glorious perfection.

Vanbrugh's palace design is magnificent, perhaps a ttle overwhelming, but the fantastic 2500 acre park as absorbed it effortlessly.

There is far too much to describe here, but nongst all the grandeur, there is the small room here Winston Churchill was born. Also make sure at you see the splendid monument of the First Duke nd Duchess of Marlborough by Rysbrack in the chapel.

CASSINGTON

(26—SE) (4 miles South of Woodstock)
centred upon a pleasantly wide green, with the short pire of its Norman church looking out across to rooded Wytham Hill, close to the confluence of the ovely River Evenlode with the Thames. The church is ull of good things, with plenty of Norman work, leasing old woodwork, medieval glass and wall paint ings, and an atmosphere of the past flavoured by assington's proximity to the medieval University of Oxford.

CHURCH HANBOROUGH

(26—NE) (3 miles South West of Woodstock)
mall village with a pretty little Victorian school house nd a wonderfully 'atmospheric' church. This has a all, slender spire, and there are yew trees lining the ath to the large north porch, which shelters a fine Norman doorway. The interior, with its old stone oors, is full of character, and there is an interesting 5th century rood screen and a roof of the same period upported on attractive corbel figures.

Bladon Church

Blenheim Palace

Blenheim Park

Blenheim Park

Effigy at North Leigh

Mosaic Pavement, North Leigh Roman Villa

South Leigh Church

COMBE

(26—NW) (2 miles West of Woodstock) Small village to the west of Blenheim Park, with the attractive Cockerel Inn looking across a wide tree shaded green towards the church, which lies a short distance below it. This is a charming little building with a vaulted north porch and Perpendicular doorway opening on to old stone flagged floors. Interesting items include a medieval stone pulpit built into the wall (an unusual feature), beautifully carved 15th century font, a triple sedilia and a richly coloured 'Doom' painting.

There is a public footpath to Woodstock, crossing the northern part of Blenheim Park, passing the great 'Column of Victory' (Map ref. **A**). Those coming to Combe by car from Long Hanborough will find a delightful resting place where the road crosses the River Evenlode (Map ref. **B**).

EAST END

(26—NW) (3 miles South West of Woodstock) Hamlet near North Leigh Roman Villa (P 121), with a warm and friendly little inn, the Leather Bottle.

EYNSHAM

(26—SE) (5 miles South of Woodstock) There are several pleasant houses and inns in this quiet little town, and in the market square there is an emaciated, iron-bound cross. Opposite the cross is Eynsham church, with many excellent Perpendicular features including a solid tower and a north porch with a priest's chamber above.

In the fields beyond the church, the Anglo-Saxons built a Benedictine monastery but although this grew to be an important establishment in the Middle Ages, no trace now remains.

FREELAND

(26—NW) (3 miles South West of Woodstock) A long straggle of unexceptional houses relieved only by a pleasantly austere little Weslyan chapel (1805) and a Victorian church, rectory and school.....all the work of J.P. Pearson, the architect of Truro Cathedral. The interior of this church is in his usually handsome style, and is well worth looking at. There is a narrow lane from here to Church Hanborough, with pleasing views of the latter's tall spire.

LONG HANBOROUGH

(26—NE) (2 miles South West of Woodstock) Is stretched out along the busy A 4095, with much modern development. However the George and Dragon looks pleasant, and there is a quiet green beside the road northwards to Combe, overlooked by the Swan Inn.

NORTH LEIGH

(26—NW) (2½ miles North East of Witney) A sprawling village with much modern development. The interesting portion lies to the north, with a character inn (dated 1783) called the Harcourt Arms and the church not far beyond, beside a handsome 17th century rectory. The interesting church has an exceptionally beautiful north aisle chapel, with stone screen and vaulting, and an altar tomb with effigies. See also the 'Doom' wall paintings over the chancel arch.

There is an attractive bridle-path southwards, beside Eynsham Park, to the A 40, and a footpath beyond it to South Leigh (P 121).

MAP 26   120

NORTH LEIGH ROMAN VILLA

(26—NW) (3½ miles West of Woodstock)
A pleasant quarter mile walk down from the road to the wooded banks of the River Evenlode brings us to this interesting Roman site. North Leigh was originally excavated in 1813 when 60 rooms surrounding a court-yard were revealed. Only one mosaic pavement visible, but this is excellent.

SOUTH LEIGH

(26—SW) (2 miles South East of Witney)
A scattered village just above the flat meadow country of the lower Windrush, with a bright and cheerful inn, the Mason's Arms and a small church at the end of a quiet cul-de-sac. There is a little priest's doorway with a cross carved on its tympanum, and a decidedly uncheerful series of 'Doom' paintings.

Stanton Harcourt Church

STANTON HARCOURT

(26—SW) (4½ miles South East of Witney)
A most attractive village containing the remains of a mansion built by the Harcourts in the 15th century, vacated by them in the 18th century, and now partly restored. Do not miss the magnificent Harcourt chapel in the church (for details, see Oxford Country by Car).

STONESFIELD

(26—NW) (3 miles West of Woodstock)
Compact village on a hilly site above the Evenlode valley, with memories of the quarries and pits that provided the well known Stonesfield Cotswold stone tiles. There are three inns, a minute village lock-up, and a warm little church, with a 'Decorated' chancel arch and south arcade, some medieval glass and a beautiful triptych reredos in the south aisle chapel.

Swinford Bridge

SWINFORD BRIDGE

(26—SE) (½ mile South East of Eynsham)
Walk down on to the tow-path to appreciate this splendid 18th century toll-bridge over the Thames. Walk a few yards downstream to Swinford Lock, or a mile and a half upstream to Pinkhill Lock, to watch a boat or two being 'locked through' on their way up to Lechlade, or down to Oxford. There is also sailing to be watched from the footpath along the southern edge of Farmoor Reservoir.

Pinkhill Lock

WOODSTOCK

(26—NE) (7 miles North East of Witney)
Owes its properous charm to the kings who had a manor here, to the Churchills, who earned the reward of Blenheim, to the glovers and their trade, and to the tourists, whose requirements are cared for with a dignity so often lacking in towns of such popularity.

From the main road to the massive park gate, Woodstock has a wonderful assortment of 17th and 18th century houses. The dignified Town Hall was built at the Duke's expense in 1766 and makes a perfect foil for the cosier charms of the Bear Hotel.

The church has a splendid 18th century tower in the Classical style, which belies its interesting medieval interior. Opposite the church, behind the town stocks, is Fletcher's House, which houses the Oxford City and County Museum. This contains a series of displays depicting life and work in Oxfordshire....very worthwhile.

House with Shutters, Woodstock

MAP 26

MAP 21 continued from P 101.

UPTON HOUSE

(21—NE) (6 miles North West of Banbury)
A William and Mary mansion with wide lawns leading to a most attractive series of terraced gardens and ornamental lakes in the valley below. The house, which was given to the National Trust by the 2nd Viscount Bearsted, contains his outstanding collection of pictures and porcelain. It is impossible to refer to this in detail but it contains works by Bosch, the Brueghels, Holbein, Rembrandt, Van Dyck, Canaletto, Goya, El Greco, Tiepolo, Tintoretto, Constable, Hogarth, Reynolds, Romney, Sartorius and Stubbs.

Do not miss a visit to this fabulous treasure house.

WHICHFORD

(21—SW) (5 miles North of Chipping Norton)
This lies below the hills, with a wide green overlooked by the little Norman Knight Inn. The early 18th century rectory is one of the most elegant country buildings one could wish to encounter and the church close by is equally attractive. See especially the alabaster relief of John Merton, a 16th century rector, and the coffin lid of Sir John Mohun.

WINDERTON

(21—NW) (8 miles West of Banbury)
Attractively sited village overlooking Brailes and the Feldon country, with an unusually fine Victorian church (1878). This has a very grand apsidal chancel enriched with alternative bands of Hornton and white freestone.

MAP 23 continued from P 109.

WITNEY

(23—SE) (7 miles East of Burford)
Pleasant old cloth town, prosperous since the days of Edward III from the making of blankets... an industry which grew apace in the Industrial Revolution and which is still very active today. The mills here are certainly not cast in Blake's 'dark Satanic' mould, and were founded by the Early family over three centuries ago.

Witney's streets run south to the little 17th century Butter Cross, and beyond this is a fine tree bordered green overlooked by lovely 17th and 18th century houses, and terminated by a tall spired church. There are plenty of interesting features within, although the Victorians were over zestful in their restoration.

There is a fascinating Farm Museum, at Cogges Manor Farm, to the immediate south-east of Witney, off the B 4022. This is complete with period farm machinery, working kitchens with dairy, and some livestock.

WYCHWOOD FOREST

(23—NW and NE) (To South West of Charlbury)
In medieval times this was a great royal forest extending from the Glyme valley near Enstone (Map 22) southwards to the Thames near Stanton Harcourt (Map 26), and from Taynton (Map 20) in the west to the Cherwell valley in the east. Since then the parks of Ditchley, Blenheim, Cornbury and Eynsham have been carved out of the forest, and most of the remainder cleared for farming. The Forest is therefore now confined to a triangle between Charlbury, Finstock and Leafield. There appears to be virtually no public access, but the road south from Ranger's Lodge (23—NW) to Leafield, has great woodlands to its east side for almost three miles and is very beautiful.

MAP 24 continued from P 113.

WIGGINTON

(24—SW) (6 miles South West of Banbury)
Quiet village above the little river Swere, with a church containing several items of interest. See especially the medieval stone seat with swan at the finial of the arch above it, and also the lovely 15th century roof to the nave.

WROXTON

(24—NW) (3 miles West of Banbury)
This village is full of thatched stone cottages, so typical of the Oxfordshire Cotswolds, where the stone is less suitable for splitting into tiles, than it is further to the south and west. Each roofing method has its own merits, but how pleasant these cottages look with their climbing roses and small gardens.

Wroxton Abbey, a fine 17th century mansion, built by Sir William Pope, is owned by the Farleigh Dickinson University of New Jersey, and its gardens and grounds have been beautifully restored. Its builder, Sir William Pope lies with his wife in a beautiful canopied tomb in the nearby church. This 14th century building also contains an elegant monument by John Flaxman to George III's Prime Minister, Lord North.

MAP 25 continued from P 117.

WESTCOTT BARTON and MIDDLE BARTON

(25—NE) (5½ miles North of Woodstock)
Now consists of one village strung out along the B 4030, just to the north of the little River Dorne, Modern housing development appears to be spoiling Middle Barton's quiet stream-side. There is a pleasant inn, called the Fox, and a church with small pinnacled Perpendicular tower. This has been over-restored, but it does have a 15th century rood screen (a relatively rare survival in these parts).

WOOTTON

(25—SE) (2 miles North of Woodstock)
Attractive village whose steep narrow streets climb up from the bridge over the Glyme. St. Mary's church has a pleasingly plain tower, and a beautiful 13th century south porch.

Why is the inn at Wootton called the Killingworth Castle? It appears that a 17th century owner named Killingworth decided to perpetuate his name by changing the title of the Inn, so please do not search for fortifications hereabouts!